EATING FOR EXCELLENCE

Sheri Rose Shepherd shares her original recipes, her offbeat humor, and her motivational skills in this lively cookbook. This book is for any woman who wants to eat well, have fun, and not fe

3-487-0

D1278310

7 WAYS TO BUILD A BETTER YOU

In this exciting video series, Sheri Rose Shepherd uses humor, heartwarming stories, and God's Word to teach emotional, physical, relational, and spiritual excellence. In just seven weekly sessions, you'll discover how to get out of the mindset of mediocrity and enter into the spirit of excellence. The Seven Ways series is fun, motivating, inspiring, and easy to apply to everyday life.

video series: ISBN 1-57673-607-5 (includes study guide)
facilitator's guide: ISBN 1-57673-604-0
study guide: ISBN 1-57673-606-7
audio series: ISBN 1-57673-603-2

FIT FOR EXCELLENCE

Fit for Excellence audio of Sheri's bestselling book.
audio: ISBN 1-57673-451-X

7 WAYS *to* BUILD *a* BETTER YOU

SHERI ROSE SHEPHERD

Multnomah Publishers® *Sisters, Oregon*

SEVEN WAYS TO BUILD A BETTER YOU
published by Multnomah Publishers, Inc.
© 1999 by Sheri Rose Shepherd
International Standard Book Number: 1–57673–557–5

Cover photograph by Tamara Reynolds
Design by Steve Shepherd

Scripture quotations are from:
Holy Bible, New Living Translation (NLT)
©1996. Used by permission of Tyndale House Publishers, Inc.
ALL RIGHTS RESERVED
Also quoted: *The Holy Bible*, New International Version (NIV)
©1973, 1984 by International Bible Society,
used by permission of Zondervan Publishing House
New American Standard Bible (NASB) ©1960, 1977, 1995
by the Lockman Foundation. Used by permission.
The Emphasized Bible, New Translation, Joseph Bryant
Rotherham (RHM) ©1959, 1994 by Kregel Publications
The Holy Bible, King James Version (KJV)

Multnomah is a trademark of Multnomah Publishers, Inc., and
is registered in the U.S. Patent and Trademark Office.
The colophon is a trademark of Multnomah Publishers, Inc.
Printed in the United States of America

ALL RIGHTS RESERVED
No part of this publication may be reproduced, stored in a retrieval
system, or transmitted, in any form or by any means—electronic, mechanical, photocopying,
recording, or otherwise—
without prior written permission.

For information:
MULTNOMAH PUBLISHERS, INC.
POST OFFICE BOX 1720
SISTERS, OREGON 97759

Library of Congress Cataloging-in-Publication Data
Shepherd, Sheri Rose, 1961-
   Seven ways to build a better you/by Sheri Rose Shepherd
      p. cm.
ISBN 1-57673-557-5 (alk. paper)
   1. Christian women—Religious life.   I. Title.
BV4527.S423 1999
248.8'43—dc21   99-047963

99 00 01 02 03 04 — 10 9 8 7 6 5 4 3 2 1

T A B L E   O F   C O N T E N T S

ACKNOWLEDGMENTS

I want to thank the wonderful staff of Multnomah for making this book possible. Don Jacobson, thank you for setting a godly example of what it means to dedicate a publishing company to our Lord Jesus Christ. Jeff Gerke, thank you for your patience, expertise, and time you've invested in the book. Jeff Pederson, thank you for your leadership, encouragement, and your great gift of marketing and managing your authors so well. Thank you to my special friend Rochelle Pederson, for your incredible gift of serving and encouraging—and of laughing at my jokes even when they're not funny.

To my husband, Steven, I love you for all that you are and all that you help me to be. To my son Jacob Andrew, when you live on your own, may you live the same life of excellence you live today. Jacob, you are a wonderful blessing to me. And to my new baby daughter, Emily Joy, I pray I can be an example of what this book teaches for you to learn from.

And mostly to my Lord and Savior Jesus Christ, thank You for taking my past hurts, mistakes, and experiences, and allowing me the privilege of ministering to others.

To all who read this book, may you be encouraged, educated, and motivated to live a life of excellence.

P R E F A C E

W elcome to an exciting and enlightening journey toward
excellence. In the next seven chapters we are going to
go beyond the ordinary and enter into the excellence zone. Every
one of us has a desire to live an excellent life. However, we find
ourselves battling between a mind-set of mediocrity and a spirit
of excellence.

In *Seven Ways to Build a Better You* we are going to use the
"Master's Plans" to build a better you physically, emotionally,
relationally, and spiritually. We're also going to make seven
choices that will change our lives both now and in eternity.

As you go through this building program, please use every
tool to build your foundation. Keep in mind there are two ways to
build: an easy way (our own human way) and an excellent way
(God's way). Second Timothy 2:19a (NIV) says, "God's solid foundation stands firm." We're going to take the excellent way.

As we build, may God give you the wisdom to understand
His plan, the strength to build, and the desire for excellence.

Enjoy your journey!

1

It's Not Where You Start.... It's Where You Finish

S heri Rose, you are a born loser." My English teacher leaned lower over my desk. "And you are never going to amount to anything."

Judging from what she had to go on, she was probably right about me. If you look at the picture on the back of this book, you'll get a glimpse of what she was looking at. I was only sixteen, but I had already made so many bad choices. I had gotten involved with the wrong crowd. I had gotten into drugs. I had started turning to food for comfort. I was sixty pounds overweight. To top it off for this English teacher, I was dyslexic in an age when there was no such term. No wonder she was frustrated with me.

But the one grammar lesson she couldn't teach me was God's. God says, "Don't put a period where I put a comma."

God has a plan for every life He creates! Unfortunately, I didn't know the author of my life when I was a young girl. But He knew me. Today, my painful past has been turned into a purpose. I live to motivate, educate, and encourage all to live a life of excellence.

It isn't where you start that matters. It's where you finish that counts. Today, I'm blessed to be an author, a speaker, a wife, and a mother of two. I'm living proof that with God, all things are possible!

LET'S TALK TRIALS AND TRIBULATION

Take the biblical story of Joseph. Joseph was a young boy who had a special call of God on his life. He had ten brothers who were out to destroy him. But he had a father who loved him and believed in him. These ten brothers wasted their time trying to tear down Joseph's life rather than build up their own lives. Jealousy and cruelty can destroy us internally and externally—and eternally.

Joseph's brothers thought they had accomplished their mission when they sold him into slavery and lied to cover their sin by telling their father he was killed. When you choose to follow God and live a life of excellence, there will always be people who will try to tear down your foundation rather than rebuild their own. However, there will be more who will be influenced, motivated, and inspired by your excellent life.

Joseph's story could have ended in bitterness and resentment. But Joseph knew God's master plan was bigger than his pain or circumstances. This story has an incredible finish, but it gets worse before it gets better.

The captain of the guard of Egypt who bought Joseph saw that Joseph was an incredible worker and that God's favor was with him. So he made him his right-hand man and gave him charge over all of his possessions. Joseph was a handsome, strong, responsible man, and the captain's wife was physically attracted to him. So she tried to seduce him. But Joseph, being a godly man, rejected her. The captain's wife told her husband that Joseph had attempted to rape her. Joseph was thrown into prison—for a crime he never committed.

Okay, let's put this story on pause. You're probably thinking, where was God in all of this, and how could all these bad things happen to such a good godly person? The answer is that God was with Joseph all along. He was building Joseph's character through these hardships into what it would have to be in order to carry out the plans He had for him. God is building Joseph's faith during this time. He's building the foundation of his life of legacy that has and will strengthen all who read about it!

Back to Egypt. God had given Joseph the supernatural ability to interpret dreams. Up to this point, that ability had seemed useless at best. To be honest, since his dreams had been what irritated his brothers so much (Genesis 37:19), this ability had been nothing but trouble. However, this special gift was about to be opened in God's perfect time.

When Pharaoh started having a horrible recurring nightmare, he sought desperately for someone who could interpret it. No one could help him, not even his magicians or wise men. His cupbearer—recently released from the dungeon—informed him that a prisoner named Joseph could interpret dreams. Pharaoh sent for Joseph.

When Joseph heard the dream, he told Pharaoh that seven years of plenty were coming, followed by seven years of famine.

Joseph suggested that grain be laid aside in the years of plenty against the years of scarcity. Pharaoh listened to Joseph. When the famine hit, Egypt was ready. Joseph became a hero in the land.

But Joseph's story doesn't end there. Joseph's brothers show up on the scene during the famine. They don't recognize him, but he sure recognizes them. If Joseph ever wanted to get even with his brothers, this was his chance.

But Joseph did something even better than getting revenge; he looked at them and said, "You meant evil against me, but God meant it for good in order to bring about this present result, to preserve many people alive" (Genesis 50:20, NASB). Joseph knew God's purpose was greater than his pain.

There will always be obstacles in the way of your goals, people in the way of God's purpose for your life, and circumstances that give God opportunities to show His sovereignty.

God has a "master" plan for every life He creates. My favorite Scripture is "'For I know the plans I have for you,' declares the LORD, 'plans to prosper you and not to harm you, plans to give you hope and a future'" (Jeremiah 29:11, NIV). That was certainly Joseph's story, and God wants it to be your story, too.

SWEET IRONY

I was recently invited to be the keynote speaker for a group of nine thousand teachers at the state capital of California, Sacramento, which is where I lived until I was twelve. Being a former D student who never went to college and didn't take school seriously, the prospect was a nightmare. I was positive that all nine thousand of them were going to be grading my speech or reading a book while I was talking, which is a speaker's nightmare.

As I was sitting on the stage of the Sacramento Memorial Auditorium next to seven other impressive-looking speakers, I felt distinctly out of place. I realized I was the only woman sitting up there, and the only person who was not well educated. But there I was. The words of that English teacher came out loud and clear.

It occurred to me that I had been in that same auditorium years before but as a completely different person. I grew up in Sacramento. When I was in eighth grade, I was in that auditorium doing LSD and worshiping a rock band. Twenty years later, God brought me back to the exact spot to share what Jesus Christ can do in a life and to encourage teachers about how their words can make a difference in the lives of students like me.

When it was my turn, I got up and encouraged those teachers to use their influence and words to impact their students for good. I'm so thankful I did not allow my bad experience with one English teacher to stop me from encouraging nine thousand.

Don't put a period where God has a comma. You don't know what He's got planned for your life. Or anyone else's.

I've learned there is great power in the way we see ourselves. And the way we see ourselves is the way we tend to understand God. This especially affects those of us who have been raised in painful situations. I come from a background of five blended families. My parents have been married and divorced three times each.

So I had never seen a marriage that worked. I was very confused about what God had for my life and how He was going to work things out. When I was young, I was so consumed with my own problems that I never thought about God. Being raised Jewish, I certainly never considered Jesus as the answer to my problems.

Because I didn't have the support I needed at home, I looked for it in my peers. The naturals, the ones who were the easiest to identify with, were the people on the same collision course I was on. I found myself bonding with the wrong people and going down a destructive path. And I spent a lot of time blaming my parents for the bad choices I was making.

When I was sixteen, I'd done so many drugs and had abused LSD so badly I almost lost my life from an overdose. When I was brought home from the hospital, I was a mess. I'll never forget when my second mother, my stepmother, walked into the room and asked me, "Sheri Rose, how long are you going to blame your past for the choices you make today? There's nothing you can do to change your past. But the choices you make today can change your future."

In the next several chapters we're going to talk about choosing the right tool to build an excellent foundation spiritually, physically, emotionally, and relationally. I'm excited to share with you the seven key things I learned through God's Word and personal experience that gave me personal victory in my life. With them, it won't matter where you started in life. What will matter for you is the wonderful place where you finish.

STUDY WORK

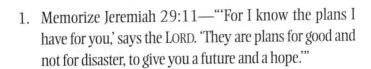

1. Memorize Jeremiah 29:11—"'For I know the plans I have for you,' says the LORD. 'They are plans for good and not for disaster, to give you a future and a hope.'"

2. What are your hopes and dreams for the future? One year from now? Five years?

3. Write down your prayer requests. Take a moment to pray about these.

4. In what ways do you want to build a better you?

5. Write your hopes and dreams in a prayer to God.

6. Ask God if your hopes and dreams are in His master plan for your life.

7. Pray for Him to change your plans and dreams to line up with His.

8. Pray for Him to show you how to start building a better you.

9. Write down what He reveals to you.

10. Write down what you can do this week to start building a better you.

Remember:

1. Don't put a period where God puts a comma.
2. It's not where you start.... It's where you finish.
3. God has a plan for you (Jeremiah 29:11).

My prayer for you:

Psalm 20:4–5—"May he grant your heart's desire and fulfill all your plans. May we shout for joy when we hear of your victory, flying banners to honor our God. May the LORD answer all your prayers."

2

Emotionally Free

Seven Keys to Freedom from Emotional Pain

God says His Word sets prisoners free. As you learn the seven keys to freedom from emotional pain, apply them to your life and break free from your prison of emotional pain.

When I first started sharing my victory story, I would tell people that I found Jesus and my life was magically changed in a moment, because I thought that was the way that you were supposed to share your testimony. I mean, once you're a Christian, I thought you weren't supposed to tell anybody you had any problems or you would make God look bad.

The more I studied God's Word, I began to realize that God is a God of truth and that it's truth that actually sets someone free. I discovered God wanted me to learn to be truthful with Him first and then to be truthful with others. He's only glorified in truth. And so I had to go through some painful circumstances while I was a Christian. The keys in this chapter were birthed out of my own personal pain. I had to learn that He is God, and I am not. He is in control, and I don't need to be. For me, that was a painful lesson to learn.

FALLING FOR THE WIN

When I was nineteen, I entered my first beauty pageant. My mother was a beauty queen, and my father, who hosted beauty pageants, was a disc jockey in Hollywood. So I grew up in the beauty pageant world. I had always dreamed of wearing a big, beautiful crown.

I entered the Miss San Jose pageant. At this point, I had just lost sixty pounds and gotten off drugs, so this was a big deal for me. The pageant directors told the girls to smile and wave at the judges. There I was, wearing an evening gown and walking down the runway. I was so proud to be there. I did that little figure-eight wave just like they taught me in rehearsal. I walked toward the judges, smiling so pretty. And walked right off the end of the runway.

The audience was dead silent. You can imagine that was probably my most embarrassing moment.

There I was, on the floor, underneath the judges' table, but believe it or not, there was something inside me that said, *I still want to win.* So I straightened out my ripped evening gown— ignored my pain from falling off the stage—and crawled back on the runway. Then I looked at the judges and said, "I just wanted you to remember me!"

I won that pageant. They said if I could pull myself out of that situation, I could probably pull myself out of anything Miss San Jose had to offer that year.

The moral of the story is, it's not how you *act*, but how you *react* that makes the difference. That day I learned that when I fall down, I can get back up again. A winner isn't someone who always says or does everything right. A winner is someone who gets back up again. If you've fallen or someone's pushed you down in life, take the next seven steps and get up and win!

KEY #1: GO TO GOD

The first key to freedom from a prison of emotional pain is to go to God to get the key. In Psalm 146:7b, the Bible says, "The LORD frees the prisoners." And John 8:36 says, "So if the Son sets you free, you will indeed be free." Many of us will go for help to everybody and everything but God. We'll go to food. We'll go to materialism. We'll go to our house. We'll go to our children. We'll go to anybody we can talk to.

Have you noticed that we will tell perfect strangers in a grocery store line more about our personal problems than we'll tell God in prayer? How many times have you shared with your hairdresser, your manicurist, the dry cleaning lady, or your kid's friends your personal problems? We'll go to everyone else, but we won't bow down to the One who can hand us the key to set us free. We need to learn to go to God.

The Bible does not say, "Be anxious for everything and let your requests be known to anyone who will listen to you." It says, "Be anxious for *nothing*, but in everything by prayer and supplication with thanksgiving let your requests be made known to *God*" (Philippians 4:6, NASB, emphasis mine).

God says He is a jealous God. When we go to anyone else, even another Christian, *before* we go to Him, He's jealous. He's not going to grant that request because He wouldn't get the glory. When we look elsewhere for freedom, He's not going to set us free. The only true freedom is in Him.

That's what I call playing our own god. Proverbs 14:12 says, "There is a path before each person that seems right, but it ends in death." If someone has hurt you, it feels right to retaliate. It seems right to divorce when your spouse has let you down. It seems right to throw out the one rebellious kid and focus on the one that's good. There's always a way that seems right, that seems fair. But in the end, it may lead to destruction.

I've learned that God is the only one who can be strong in our weakness. He's the faithful one. He's the one who heals us when we're hurting. He's our protection when we are in trouble. He's the power when we need a miracle. Every time I have turned to everything but the Lord to try to fix my problems, I have strayed. I have walked right back into that prison of pain. How many times does God have to show us that He is God and we are not, and that He wants to handle our problems for us?

God gives us specific instructions for every area of our lives. Many of us don't even realize it. We have beautiful Bibles sitting on our coffee tables, but we rarely open them. We've never allowed the Word of life to empower our lives. We can say the right words. We can give the right answers. We can act spiritual—and we're good at acting, aren't we? But remember, it's not how we act, but how we react that counts.

I have learned that when we don't go to God, we're not going to react the way we need to. I've learned that God wants us to react to Him. Go to Him to get the key, and you will be free.

KEY #2: HIT YOUR HURTS HEAD-ON

The second key to freedom is to remove your guard and hit your hurts head-on. This is difficult for a lot of us to do. We feel safer having a guard over our hearts, even with God. And because many of us have not had good relationships with our fathers, it's hard for us to relate to our heavenly Father. It's hard for us to remove the guard and go head-on with Him into a battle.

I have learned that the greater the battle in your life, the greater the victory is going to be. So think of it this way: the more problems you have, the more you're blessed. Think of the greater victories you're going to have to talk about in the days to come.

God has designed a winning wardrobe to hit your battles head-on. It's found in Ephesians 6:13–16. He gave us a belt of truth, armor of righteousness, shoes of peace, a hat of salvation, the shield of faith, the sword of the Spirit which is the word of God, and the power of prayer. But if we don't put the wardrobe on, if we go to battle without it, we're not going to win.

Did you notice that in that whole winning wardrobe, God didn't put anything on our backside? Why did He keep us open on our backside? Because He never intended us to run from our problems. He gave us everything we need to face whatever hits our lives head-on.

If you don't hit your hurts head-on, you hide them in your heart. And whatever is inside you will control you. God doesn't remove emotional pain if you don't deal with it. You can pretend that things are okay. You can act spiritual. But when there's pain hidden in your heart, until you give it to Him, He's not going to remove it.

If it's spiritual to pretend everything is okay, then why are so many Christians depressed? Why are so many Christian people disillusioned about the power of their faith? God is waiting to show His power, but we have to remove that guard and hit our hurts head-on. Our heavenly Father sees our hidden hurts, but He cannot (or will not) heal what we will *not* reveal.

James 4:2 says, "The reason you don't have what you want is that you don't ask God for it." He's waiting for us to open up whatever is in our hearts. He heals broken hearts when He has all the pieces, not some of the pieces.

God uses our emotions, bad or good, to reveal the condition of our spirits. Emotions aren't bad things. There are two thousand references in the Bible to the emotions of God. He wants to use our emotions to reveal what's going on inside of us. Many times He sends us warning signs—signs like compulsive eating, depression, anxiety, fear, a pattern of destructive relationships. But we just continue to sail through life ignoring the signs.

It's like we're in a car with warning lights flashing on the dash. But every time a warning sign comes up, we put a piece of black tape over it. Some of us put a piece of gold tape and a rhinestone on it because it looks prettier. But we cover them up. Have you ever noticed that the car always breaks down at the wrong time? Have you ever exploded emotionally at the wrong time? You probably know exactly what I'm talking about. And then we blame God.

But He says, "I tried to warn you. I put up warning signs, but you didn't come to Me. You went to everybody but Me. You were afraid to remove that guard and let Me heal the hidden hurts that were in your heart." If we don't deal with pain, the pain will deal with us. And it will deal with our relationships. There's nothing to be afraid of with God. He is the only one who can set us free.

About two years after I was saved, my eating disorder and my depression returned. I thought that it was just an attack from Satan because I was a Christian. I felt that if I could just pray and have others pray for me and if I could just bind Satan from coming against my mind and my body that I would be healed from this eating disorder. But no matter how much I prayed or how many people prayed for me, God did not release me from it. You can imagine how discouraged I was.

What I finally realized was that there were warning lights going off in my life. There were things I had not given to God. One of those things was my relationship with my mother.

I know my mother loved me to the best of her ability. But because she wasn't loved by her mother, she had a tough time expressing love to me, which left me feeling very lonely and insecure. So I withdrew from her, and she withdrew from me. By the time I was married, my mom and I had no relationship whatsoever.

When I got pregnant with our little boy, Jacob, I wanted to have a relationship with my mother. But I was afraid to hit my hurts head-on. I had not spoken with her in so long, and it was such an unresolved relationship. I wasn't sure if I should hit it head-on, or if I should just leave it and let it go.

But God would not release me from wanting that love and

acceptance from my mother. And even though I had a wonderful stepmother who loved me greatly, I still wanted to make my relationship with my mom right. I didn't have peace in my heart. I wanted to tell my mom that I was pregnant with my baby. I wanted her to be a part of my life, but I was so afraid. I finally wrote her a letter letting her know I was pregnant.

A few weeks later, I received a package in the mail from my mom. I was so excited. I thought it was a baby gift. It wasn't. It was my baby shoes, my birth certificate, and my baby photos. The note said, "I wish you'd never been born. You've caused me greater pain than anything else in my life."

I was devastated. I had taken a chance. I had removed the guard from my heart. I had hit a hurt head-on—and gotten blasted.

I started wondering if that letter had been the right thing to do. Should I have trusted God by contacting my mom? "Lord, how can I forgive her when she doesn't forgive me? It wasn't my fault my parents' marriage didn't work out. It wasn't my fault she didn't have a mother to love her." I was crying out to God, "I didn't do anything wrong!" But I felt the Lord say to me in my spirit, "Neither did I, but I went to a cross for you."

Through a bucket of tears and the strength of the Lord, I wrote a second letter to my mom. I asked her to forgive me for whatever I had done that had caused her to feel such great pain and regret for having given birth to me. In writing that letter and giving it to my mom, God not only healed my eating disorder and lifted my depression, He restored my relationship with my mother. Today, my mother is a born-again Christian, and it is as if there was never any pain in our relationship.

Now, this didn't happen immediately. When my mom and I were brought back together, it wasn't an immediate—"poof"—magically better situation. Forgiveness, when there's emotional pain involved, takes time. But what happens when you hit something head-on, when you go to the person and make things right, is that, even if they don't receive it, even if the relationship doesn't change, you remove the root of bitterness that was growing in *your* life.

It took over seven years before my mom actually felt comfortable with me and I felt comfortable with her. But the root of bitterness had been pulled. That is part of the "losing a battle to win the war" dynamic in your life.

I still had more things to deal with. Even though God had healed my eating disorder, I still had a lot of insecurities. I was still very uncomfortable receiving love from others. I realized I was like that because I had a father who loved me with a toxic love.

Toxic love is different from God's love. Toxic love makes the heart sick. And even though my father loved me in his worldly way to the best of his ability, his type of love—his temper, his hurtful words—damaged my spirit and made me afraid to love others and to trust people. It affected my marriage.

I finally realized I needed to set some boundaries with my father. I faced him head-on. I let him know how much I loved him and how much I wanted him in my life. But I also told him that if he was going to continue speaking badly to me and loving me with a toxic love, he would *not* have any part of my life or my child's life.

If you continue being victimized by a toxic love, you're no longer a victim, you're a volunteer. God valued you so much He gave His only Son for you. Do you think, then, that He wants someone to love you with a toxic love? Even Jesus set boundaries. So I drew the line. I said, "You will not talk to me in a manner that crushes my spirit." When I turned to him and hit it head-on, he respected me and realized he was going to have to make some changes, or he wasn't going to be a part of my life or his grandson's.

It's okay to set boundaries. When God says, "Turn the other cheek when someone hits you," He does not mean for you to stay there until your face is black and blue. He means do not respond to them the way they respond to you. Show them God's way, God's love. Then get out of the way. If you are being victimized, you need to face toxic love head-on.

KEY #3: DON'T BE AFRAID TO BREAK FREE

The third key to freedom is to not be afraid to break free.

> Do not be afraid, for I have ransomed you. I have called you by name; you are mine. When you go through deep waters and great trouble, I will be with you. When you go through rivers of difficulty, you will not drown! When you walk through the fire of oppression, you will not be burned up; the flames will not consume you. (Isaiah 43:1–2)

Some of us are afraid to break free. We're more comfortable covered in our chains. At salvation, God unlocks the door. But we have to remove the chains and get up and walk in the promises of God. I've met more people who walk right back into the situation they were in over and over and over again because they are more comfortable in a prison of pain, because freedom feels foreign to them.

The greatest comfort is being covered in God's love. We don't need to be afraid to break free. Many people stay bound in abusive relationships, unproductive situations, and jobs they hate. Life is too short to sit in a prison of pain. God wants to set you free.

Second Chronicles 20:15b says, "For the battle is not yours, but God's." Many of us are afraid because we think we're going to have to hit something head-on in our own power. First John 4:4 (NASB) says, "You are from God, little children, and have overcome them; because greater is He who is in you than he who is in the world."

John 14:27 says, "I am leaving you with a gift—peace of mind and heart. And the peace I give isn't like the peace the world gives. So don't be troubled or afraid." Peace in what? Peace in knowing God is in control of your situation. Peace in knowing He will always be with you. Peace in knowing He works all things together for good for those who are in Christ Jesus—not some things—but *all* things. Romans 8:28 (NASB) doesn't say, "All things feel good." It says, "He works all things together *for* good."

I want you to say something out loud right now: "He is God. I am not." Did you say it? Do it again. "He is God. I am not." Isn't that great? What a revelation. Don't be afraid to break free from the prison of pain and walk in freedom.

KEY #4: PRAISE THROUGH THE PAIN

How hard it is to praise God in pain! "Thank you, God. Bring me more pain. I want to be more spiritual." I've never heard any Christians praying that prayer. But in Psalm 33:1, it says, "Let the godly sing with joy to the LORD, for it is fitting to praise him."

Notice that Paul praised his way through his pain when he was in prison. And what happened? The chains fell off (Acts 16:25–26). But Paul didn't stop there. It wasn't only physical chains God broke for Paul. He told the jailer about spiritual freedom, and that man's "chains" fell away, too (Acts 16:27–34).

David praised God through the pain when he was running for his life. But what happened out of David's pain? We got the book of Psalms. How comforting that is today. God set David free because he praised Him when everything looked like it was falling apart.

> Then I will hold my head high, above my enemies who surround me. At his Tabernacle I will offer sacrifices with shouts of joy, singing and praising the LORD with music. (Psalm 27:6)

David was determined to praise God at any cost. Nothing was going to stop God's purpose from happening in his life.

I'm not saying, "Don't feel pain." I'm saying, "Praise Him

through the pain." When we praise our way through the pain, it changes our attitude. It moves God's hand. And the chains fall off. "Those who plant in tears will harvest with shouts of joy" (Psalm 126:5).

KEY #5: LET YOUR PAST TEACH YOU, NOT TORMENT YOU

God uses our past to teach us. The reason God doesn't let us forget our past is because He wants us to learn the lessons and not have to repeat them. Satan uses our past to torture us.

Peter had to get beyond the memory that he had denied Jesus three times. Paul had to let go of the fact that he had been a persecutor of Christians. He knew he was, but he had to let it go. David had to let go of the guilt of adultery and murder. Now that's a tough one to let go of. But when he repented and turned to God, he believed God would use him again.

You can't change yesterday—you can only change today. You will never be who God created you to be as long as you're living in yesterday. In Isaiah 43:18 (NIV), God says, "Forget the former things; do not dwell on the past." Hear it in Paul's words:

> No, dear friends, I am still not all I should be, but I am focusing all my energies on this one thing: Forgetting the past and looking forward to what lies ahead, I strain to reach the end of the race and receive the prize for which God, through Christ Jesus, is calling us up to heaven. (Philippians 3:13–14)

God wants to do a new thing in you but that won't happen as long as you're wallowing in the old thing. Once you've hit your hurts head-on and dealt with the pain in your life, the way to forget it is to stop talking about it.

When God rescued Shadrach, Meshach, and Abednego from the fiery furnace, they didn't even smell like smoke. The problem with a lot of us is we still stink. We walk around and talk about our past. It's one thing to talk about your past to help pull someone else out of where you've been so they can experience freedom. It's another thing to walk around complaining about everything Satan has brought against you but celebrating nothing God has done to free you.

If we act like that long enough, we're going to find ourselves right back in that prison of pain. As Lisa Bevere says, "Your past is not your future." Learn from your past. Don't let it torment you.

KEY #6: BE WHAT GOD HAS CALLED YOU TO BE

Many of us wander around saying, "I'm going to wait for when God can use me." I remember thinking I didn't have any gifts at all. I didn't think I had a purpose. I mean, I knew the Lord loved me. I knew I was born again and I loved sharing Christ, but I didn't understand that God actually had a gift inside of me He wanted to unwrap. He wants to unwrap the gift inside you, too, so it can be given away as a present to others and to Him.

Your passion is your purpose.

I remember when I was just out of high school thinking, "What do I want to be when I grow up?" Now there are many of us who are forty or fifty or sixty thinking, "What do I want to be when I grow up?" The question should be, "What do I want to be when I grow up in God?" But I remember I tried all kinds of things.

The first thing I tried was waitressing. Since I like people, money, and food, I thought that would be a good job. My very first time on the job, I accidentally dumped a spinach salad on a man's head. And because I have a wild sense of humor, I laughed hysterically in his face. Needless to say, I was fired on the spot.

Then I thought I'd try beauty college. You know, I like pretty things and makeup and doing hair, so why not? The very first day we had our practical application where we shampooed some-one's hair, I almost drowned a lady. I shot a hose right up her nose. Again, I started busting up laughing because of my sense of humor. She didn't think anything was funny about it.

There were so many things I tried. I knew no one wanted a dyslexic secretary, so I figured that one might be a little tough to accomplish. I couldn't sing, I couldn't dance, I couldn't act. The only reason I even thought about those things was because they were what you were supposed to do in beauty pageants. I could not figure out what in the world I was going to be when I grew up.

I've always had one passion—my constant need is to com-municate with people. My greatest fear is dead air. Generally speaking, I'm generally speaking—to anybody, anywhere, any-time. I didn't understand then that God had put that passion inside me and wanted me to use it to encourage others.

Finally someone said to me, "Sheri, God has done wonderful things in your life. Share it." And so I started sharing it with everybody and anybody who would listen—telling them about a relationship with God.

One night I was at a table with my husband and twenty strangers from Talbot University, the seminary my husband attended. I was sitting at the table doing what I'm always doing—talking or eating—my two favorite things in life. This woman across the table said, "I heard you were fat, Jewish, and on drugs. What happened?" Needless to say, everybody stopped crunching their croutons. All eyes were on me.

That was my first speaking engagement. I shared for the first time what God had done in my life from a truthful perspective—where He had brought me from. I remember driving home with Steve that night saying, "Thank You, God—I never have to do that again." Of course, I had no idea that God was, that night, birthing a ministry for me. Your passion is your purpose.

That very woman who had embarrassed me in front of those twenty strangers called me up a week later and asked if I would share my testimony with four hundred Christian leaders. Her speaker had canceled at a conference in Phoenix. I said, "Lady, people like me don't speak to perfect Christian leaders because Christian leaders never sin." I've matured a lot since then.

I was so afraid. I thought, "How could God use me in front of these Christian leaders?" These women were ministry directors from all over the country. There was no way I was going to go and share every mistake I'd ever made. As I was giving her my list of excuses, she interrupted me. "Sheri Rose, God didn't pull you out of that dark place for you to keep it to yourself. He pulled you out because He wants you to pull others out, too."

When God delivers us from something, He wants to use us to deliver someone else. We can be what God created us to be in spite of our circumstances. It may be that our circumstances *enhance* our ability to be what God intended us to be.

One of the most amazing opportunities God's given me has been the privilege of writing books. How many dyslexics write books? The girl whose *English* teacher said she'd never amount to anything—an author?

Little did I know that God would unwrap my passion for motivating people through the spoken and written word. Even so, it wasn't until I stopped focusing on what I couldn't do and started building my life on what God could do that I was able to confidently express myself as a speaker and an author.

Think about Joseph: hated and rejected and thrown into prison, but aware that God's purpose was greater than his pain. Not only did God use what his family did to him for good, but Joseph could confidently face his family at the end of his horrible life. I mean, the man was thrown into prison for doing what was right. But God still stuck him in a palace. Joseph could even sit before his family and say, "God turned into good what you meant for evil" (Genesis 50:20a). God can take whatever experiences you've had and use them—use you—to be a blessing for others.

Maybe you say, "I can't be what God created me to be because I'm overweight." "I can't be what God created me to be because I have too much pain." Or, "I can't be what God created me to be because I have a child who's not saved." That kind of thinking is so untrue. You need to say, "This is the day God has made for me to be what He has created me to be."

We all have different gifts. Some of us are very organized. The gift of organization—I love those people. I don't have that gift. I need to surround myself with those people. Some of us are wonderful hostesses. We love having people in our home. Others of us freak out when we're going to have someone over. Well, find someone who has the gift of hosting and throw your parties at their house. And have the organized people come over and clean it up.

No matter what gifts we have, we can all be what God created us to be. But we're our own worst enemy, aren't we? We're the ones who make all the excuses of why we can't be what God calls us to be. Ecclesiastes 11:4 tells us, "If you wait for perfect conditions, you will never get anything done."

Joseph never made excuses. He never said, "No, I can't be in the palace because I just came out of a prison. No, I can't be pharaoh's right-hand man because of the family I came from." As a matter of fact, he never even changed his attitude when he went through that trial. He trusted God. He praised Him. Unwrap the gift inside you and be who God created you to be.

KEY #7: LIVE FOR TODAY

The last key to freedom is to live for today. Many of us are bound up in emotional pain because we're living in yesterday—or in tomorrow.

Have you noticed how many of us are always in the next moment? We're at lunch with a girlfriend, but we're thinking about when we have to pick up our kids. We pick up our kids, but we're thinking about what we have to make for dinner. We go home for dinner, but we're thinking about what we have to do before we go to bed. And we wonder why we're emotionally locked up in a prison of loneliness—why we feel isolated. It's because we're never where God calls us to be. Barbara Johnson says it best: "We need to live each day as if it's our last, because one day we're going to be right."

When God healed me from my addiction to drugs, I picked up another addiction. Maybe you can relate to this one. It's called the "I'll be happy when…" syndrome. Think about it. When we're kids in high school, we say we're going to be happy when we're seniors and can rule the school.

Then when we reached our senior year, we said, "Well, I'll be happy when I can move out, and Mom and Dad can't tell me what to do." Too thick to realize we had a great life at home and didn't have to pay any bills. If you could, would you at least think about going back home today, knowing what you know now?

When we're single, we don't enjoy our single life. We say, "I'm going to be happy when God brings me a spouse." If you're married, did it work? Did marriage magically grant you happiness? If you're single, enjoy your life.

If you're looking for things to make you happy—a better marriage, thinner thighs, better eyes, better house, different circumstances—the devil will steal your joy, and you are going to feel like you're bound up in emotional pain.

Some of us live as if we'll never die. I've heard people say, "I've got so many things to do and I'm so far behind, I'll never die." Let these words from Psalm 39 be your prayer every morning when you start your day:

LORD, remind me how brief my time on earth will be. Remind me that my days are numbered, and that my life is fleeing away. My life is no longer than the width of my hand. An entire lifetime is just a moment to you; human existence is but a breath. (Psalm 39:4–5)

We always think we have tomorrow. So we get to the end of our life and feel like we haven't accomplished anything—nothing but busyness and emptiness. Can you relate? Are you always in the next place doing the next thing, never where you *are*, doing what you're doing?

My father said he was always fighting time. "I'm fighting time—I don't have time to enjoy life." We'd always tell him, "Take a breath. Enjoy life." Unfortunately, he learned too late in life that you can always make more money, but you can never buy back time. He lives with a lot of regret today because he didn't enjoy his children while they were at home.

Children aren't going to remember the bigger house and the nicer car and the nicer clothes. They are going to remember that you lived for today and that you enjoyed them. Or didn't.

Decide what's most important to you and give that your most valuable possession—time. It's most valuable because it's irreplaceable. It can't be bought back. Life isn't a dress rehearsal. We don't get another performance.

SUMMARY

Take these seven keys and unlock those prison doors. Be free. We women are notorious for beating ourselves up for feeling too emotional. We feel guilty that we are in pain and then we bury those emotions. Did you know you don't have to feel guilty for being emotional? God created you—in the image of God—to feel. The key is to let Him break you free from emotional pain to be what He's created you to be. Don't focus on what you can't do, excel in what you can do and do it!

STUDY WORK

1. Memorize Isaiah 43:1b–2—"Do not be afraid, for I have ransomed you. I have called you by name; you are mine. When you go through deep waters and great trouble, I will be with you. When you go through rivers of difficulty, you will not drown! When you walk through the fire of oppression, you will not be burned up; the flames will not consume you."

2. Write down your prayer requests. Take a moment to pray about these.

3. Write down all the things (people, food, and so on) you may have gone to, besides God, in order to attempt to free yourself from pain.

4. Write down all the emotional pain hidden in your heart. Maybe it's guilt, fear, jealousy, bitterness, resentment. Whatever it is, get it out on paper. Then give it to God.

5. Note some steps you can take toward freedom (truth, confrontation, phone call, change).

6. Go to God in prayer for the strength to take those steps.

7. Make a list of the things you're grateful for.

8. List the three most valuable lessons you've learned from your past.

9. How can you apply these lessons to your life today?

10. Make a list of things you do well (organizing, encouraging people, talking, serving, art, hosting, teaching, singing, playing with children, listening).

11. How can you use your gifts to bless those around you?

12. Complete this sentence: "I'll be happy when…"

13. Write out what you've allowed to distract you from living for today.

14. Memorize Proverbs 24:16a—"For though a righteous man falls seven times, he rises again" (NIV).

Remember:

1. Go to God to get the key.
2. Hit your hurts head-on.
3. Don't be afraid to break free.
4. Praise your way through the pain.
5. Let your past teach you, NOT torment you.
6. Be what God called you to be.
7. Live for today.

3

Excellent People Make Excellent Choices

Seven Secrets to Skillful Living

Excellent people are excellent because they make excellent choices. There are seven choices you can make that will change your life. It is truly choice, not chance, that will determine your future.

> Today I have given you the choice between life and death, between blessings and curses. I call on heaven and earth to witness the choice you make. Oh, that you would choose life, that you and your descendants might live! (Deuteronomy 30:19)

Throughout the Bible, God gives us choices. He gives us the choice to live with Him for eternity or live without Him for eternity. We can choose to hang in there, or we can choose to walk away. There is always a choice, even when we don't realize we have one. Sometimes we don't know what choices to make.

So let me say with Paul, "And now I will show you the most

excellent way" (1 Corinthians 12:31b, NIV). There's an easy way, and there's an excellent way. This is about the excellent way.

EXCELLENT CHOICE #1: CHOOSE A GOAL

Many of us wander around in life aimlessly because we have not set a goal.

> Look straight ahead, and fix your eyes on what lies before you. Mark out a straight path for your feet; then stick to the path and stay safe. Don't get sidetracked; keep your feet from following evil. (Proverbs 4:25–27)

There's nothing worse than not knowing where you're going and killing yourself to get there. So often we get sidetracked, or we get onto the wrong track because we're not following any path. We don't have a goal. We don't have a plan. "Where there is no vision, the people perish" (Proverbs 29:18a, KJV).

We need to have a vision, and we need to ask God for that vision. Go to God and ask, "Lord, what is it that You want for my life?" It needs to be more than a good idea. It needs to be a God idea. If it's a God idea and He wants to use you, then it's going to be blessed.

I want to challenge you to think about what it is God wants to use you to do. Where do you see yourself five years from now? Ten years from now? Is your daily routine going to take you where you want to be three to five years from now? Write out a goal for yourself.

So many times when we don't make a plan, we just wander around aimlessly in the desert like the Israelites did, and we never get to the Promised Land. God has a promise on your life. He has a plan for your life. But unless you make a plan and commit it to Him, you're not going to see His promises or His plan come to pass in your lifetime.

EXCELLENT CHOICE #2: CHOOSE TO USE WISDOM

In other words, choose to read life's introduction manual. The Bible is our Basic Instructions Before Leaving Earth. Ephesians 5:15–16 says, "So be careful how you live, not as fools but as those who are wise. Make the most of every opportunity for doing good in these evil days." Wisdom is knowing what to do in a situation, how to do it, and when to do it.

James 1:5 says, "If you need wisdom—if you want to know what God wants you to do—ask Him, and He will gladly tell you." It's such a simple thing. We go to everybody but God. He's the only One who can give us wisdom. And He will grant us wisdom if we ask Him to reveal what He wants us to do and if we read His Word.

> Let those who are wise understand these things.
> Let those who are discerning listen carefully. The
> paths of the LORD are true and right, and righ-
> teous people live by walking in them. But sinners
> stumble and fall along the way. (Hosea 14:9)

Often Christians don't live any differently than non-Christians because some Christians do not know God's plan.

They've never read all of it, for one thing. How can we build an excellent foundation with only a small part of the building plan? We need it all.

Choose to use wisdom. How many of our problems have been caused by our own unwise choices? It's true of me. I have learned to ask God, "Lord, what do you want me to do in this situation?" and then to be quiet enough—long enough—to hear Him answer. God has a solution for every situation in life.

EXCELLENT CHOICE #3:
CHOOSE HOW YOU WILL SPEND YOUR TIME

Ecclesiastes 3:1a (NIV) says, "There is a time for everything." Right now, you may be a mother and this is your season to spend your time with your children. Or maybe you're a single person and this is your time to forget about finding a spouse and invest whatever time has been given you into a ministry or a friend. Maybe you're a businessman and you've spent too much time at the office, and it's time for you to get focused on your family.

We all go through different seasons, so we can't make a blanket statement about how we're going to spend our time for the rest of our lives. But we can certainly look at what we have today and say, "God, how do You want me to spend my time in *this* season of my life?"

When I first started this speaking ministry, I said yes to every opportunity to minister. If a weekend was open, I filled it. Thankfully, I was blessed enough to have a godly woman named Donna Otto give me counsel. Donna has a ministry called Homemakers by Choice that encourages women to raise their children. One day she said, "When you say yes to these commitments, you're saying no to your son and your husband. So you'd better pray before you commit to something and ask God how He wants you to spend your time." I realized that if my ministry on the road was getting more time than my ministry in my home, then I was out of God's will. I wasn't spending my most valuable possession wisely.

How many times do all our good things make us miss the best thing? We love to do good things and fun things and be with friends—and those are very important—but we need to go to God first and ask Him for wisdom. "Lord, how do You want me to spend this time?" The yes you give to something can mean a no to your sleep, your spouse, and even the God you say you love but for whom you can't make any time.

You need to make excellent choices in how you invest your most valuable possession. Look at your priorities. Look at what needs to be edited out of your life so you can spend your time the way God would have you spend it.

Many of us spend more time in front of a television than we ever do having a conversation with someone. I'm not saying TV is bad. But I am saying that if you're watching soap operas all day and your husband comes home, and he doesn't make you feel bold and beautiful and young and restless, you're going to want to put him in the General Hospital. We need to be careful how we spend our time because life is short, and it's going to be over quickly.

There are three kinds of people in this world: people who make things happen, people who watch things happen, and people who get to the ends of their lives and say, "What happened?" People who invest their time wisely, who think about where they're spending God's greatest gift, do *not* live with regret. They live a life of contentment because they have invested their most precious possession in what's important to them.

My rule is I don't put things in my schedule that don't fit my priorities. We need to make a list of our priorities, asking God for wisdom. If something comes along that doesn't fit your priorities, don't commit to it. Choose wisely, for God has given you your time.

EXCELLENT CHOICE #4: CHOOSE YOUR BATTLES

Many of us don't know we have a choice. We get upset over things that don't really matter. Think about the things we waste our energy on. Save your time and energy for battles worth fighting. One of the wisest things my father ever shared with me was, "Sheri, you've got to be willing to lose some battles to win the war."

What good is winning an argument if you lose a friend? What good is winning a point if you lose a spouse or child? What are you really winning? Proverbs 20:3 tells us, "Avoiding a fight is a mark of honor; only fools insist on quarreling." What good is winning our way if we lose our witness to the world? Many of us demand our own rights—what we should get, where we should be standing in line, who should be serving us first—at the cost of losing our witness to the world.

Philippians 2:14 says, "In everything you do, stay away from complaining and arguing." You win when you fight for what's good, just, and true. Why don't we spend our time and energy fighting for souls for Christ? You win when you fight your flesh to do what's right. There's a battle worth winning.

You win if you keep your eyes focused on your goals and off the obstacles. You know what an obstacle is? An obstacle is what you notice when you take your eyes off the goal. The devil doesn't have to defeat you to win; all he has to do is distract you. He does everything he can to distract God's people from accomplishing what God has for them. And if we do not decide what battles we're going to fight and what battles we're going to leave alone, we're not going to win anything but a life of frustration. Choose your battles, even lose a few, and win the war for your life.

EXCELLENT CHOICE #5: CHOOSE YOUR WORDS

> The tongue is a flame of fire. It is full of wickedness that can ruin your whole life. It can turn the entire course of your life into a blazing flame of destruction, for it is set on fire by hell itself. People can tame all kinds of animals and birds and reptiles and fish, but no one can tame the tongue. It is an uncontrollable evil, full of deadly poison. Sometimes it praises our Lord and Father, and sometimes it breaks out into curses against those who have been made in the image of God. And so blessing and cursing come pouring out of the same mouth. Surely, my brothers and sisters, this is not right! (James 3:6–10)

Do you think God wants us to control our tongues? Think about the power of words. The Bible tells us the power of life and death is in our tongues (Proverbs 18:21). What we say, what we talk about is going to affect how we feel, how we look, and how we look to others. It's going to affect everything we do. It's going to affect the outcome of our lives. It's going to affect our relationships with our spouses, our kids, our friends. It's going to affect our witness.

Proverbs 10:32 says, "The godly speak words that are helpful, but the wicked speak only what is corrupt." Ephesians 4:29 says, "Don't use foul or abusive language. Let everything you say be good and helpful, so that your words will be an encouragement to those who hear them."

Our words tear down or they build up. They can encourage or they discourage. Our words can make or break someone's life. They can make or break a situation. The way we word things to someone can build their confidence or just wipe out their world. We have a great responsibility as Christians to choose our words. We have an opportunity to let our words be a blessing to those who hear.

I want to warn you of something else about your words. What you read, what you watch, and what you listen to will affect everything you say. Because whatever goes into your mind goes into your heart, and it comes out your mouth. Garbage in, garbage out. If you don't guard what you put into your mind, you will have no power to choose your words.

Listen to David's words: "I said to myself, 'I will watch what I do and not sin in what I say. I will curb my tongue when the ungodly are around me'" (Psalm 39:1). Notice the first thing he says: "I will watch what I *do* and not sin in what I *say*." David understood that what he did would affect what he said. I'd like to challenge you to recite the following prayer every morning for a week: "Take control of what I say, O LORD, and keep my lips sealed" (Psalm 141:3). Only God can control our tongues, so go to Him for help.

There's another thing about our mouths that we're going to have to go to God about. We women are good at this—talking too much and not listening enough to what the Lord would have us say. I've learned it's better to swallow your words before you say them than to have to eat them later. Choose your words carefully.

EXCELLENT CHOICE #6: CHOOSE YOUR FRIENDS

Proverbs 13:20 says, "Whoever walks with the wise will become wise; whoever walks with fools will suffer harm." How many of us mothers have seen how affected our kids are by those with whom they walk? Well, the same is true for adults. Surround yourself with what you want to become, because you become what you surround yourself with.

Choose friends who love God like you do. You should only be with those who don't love God if you are there to witness to them and share the love of God with them. If you are not sharing with them what God has done in your life, and they are bringing you into their world, you're becoming "of the world." That is not a relationship you should be maintaining.

Choose your friends wisely. The Bible says, "As iron sharpens iron, a friend sharpens a friend" (Proverbs 27:17). Choose friends who aren't afraid to speak the truth. Choose friends who aren't afraid to hold you accountable and to tell you what's right and wrong for your life. Choose friends who choose excellence for their lives. Choose friends you respect.

Choose friends who give good advice. Since we usually listen to our friends' advice, we need to be careful from whom we get advice. We need to look at their lives, look at their motives, and look at their maturity level in the Lord. Ecclesiastes 12:12 says, "But, my child, be warned: There is no end of opinions ready to be expressed. Studying them can go on forever and become very exhausting!" Opinions are like belly buttons—everybody has one. Free advice could cost you your life. Watch whom you take advice from.

Friends are like buttons on an elevator. They'll either bring you up or they'll bring you down. You will become what you surround yourself with, so choose your friends wisely.

EXCELLENT CHOICE #7: CHOOSE YOUR ATTITUDE

"Always be full of joy in the Lord. I say it again—rejoice!" (Philippians 4:4).

It's hard to choose your attitude if you haven't dealt with your emotional pain. You can't choose your attitude if you stuff things inside and don't give them to God. Whatever is inside of you will control you. So, if you don't apply the principles of chapter 2, you will not be able to apply the principles here. If you haven't dealt with your emotional pain, go back to chapter 2, then come back.

We need to choose our attitude. Sometimes we are pretty whiny. It's pitiful. Think about it. "I'm so tired." "I'm so sick." "Someone cut in front of me." "I didn't get what I wanted." Whine, whine, whine. "I don't know why God's not using me. I'm a Christian. Want to go to church with me?"

Jesus turned the water into wine. But He can't turn our whining into anything.

Negative thoughts don't have any power unless we empower them. Our attitudes are going to be affected by what we think about. What we think about is going to be affected by what we read and watch and what we talk about. We will become what we read and watch and talk about. So, if you want to have a good attitude from the inside out, then you will need to be careful and guard your mind and heart in Christ Jesus, following His most excellent way.

In 1 Thessalonians 5:18 the Word of God tells us, "No matter what happens, always be thankful, for this is God's will for you who belong to Christ Jesus." And Paul writes in Philippians:

> Fix your thoughts on what is true and honorable and right. Think about things that are pure and lovely and admirable. Think about things that are excellent and worthy of praise. (Philippians 4:8b)

What helps me keep a good attitude is listening to praise music. I also keep a list of my blessings on my mirror or in my daytimer. When the devil comes to tell me about the two things that are wrong, I can tell him about the ten things that are right.

Attitude is the one thing we can choose. We can't always control what happens to us, but we can control what happens *in* us. Our attitude is what exemplifies our character. It's our reactions that declare to whom we belong and how our life is going to turn out.

SUMMARY

It's exciting to know God gives us choices, isn't it? He gives us our own free will. It is truly our choices that will determine our future success. Excellent choices lead to an excellent future. Choose well.

STUDY WORK

1. Memorize Deuteronomy 30:19—"Today I have given you the choice between life and death, between blessings and curses. I call on heaven and earth to witness the choice you make. Oh, that you would choose life, that you and your descendants might live!"

2. Write down your prayer requests. Take a moment to pray about these.

3. In chapter 1 we talked about dreams and hopes. Now let's talk about goals. Make a list of some personal goals you want to accomplish in the next year. Make lists of your five-year and ten-year goals, too.

4. What needs to be your daily routine to accomplish some of these goals?

5. What are some wise choices you can make to build a better you?

6. What can be edited out of your time schedule to build a better you?

7. List some things not worth fighting about.

8. Now list some things that are worth fighting for.

9. Are there people you need to go seek forgiveness from?

10. Do the friends you spend time with reflect what you want to become?

11. Ask God what attitudes He might want you to change.

Remember:

1. Choose a goal.
2. Choose to use wisdom.
3. Choose how you will spend your time.
4. Choose your battles.
5. Choose your words.
6. Choose your friends.
7. Choose your attitude.

4

Eating for Excellence

Seven Heavenly Ways to Boost Your Energy

Have you ever been sick and tired of being sick and tired? Well, eating for excellence is not about your weight. It's not about being Barbie with a Bible. It's not about being in a pageant or being on the cover of *Fit* magazine. It's about presenting your body as a living and holy sacrifice to God. Because in 1 Corinthians 6:19–20 it says, "Or don't you know that your body is the temple of the Holy Spirit, who lives in you and was given to you by God? You do not belong to yourself, for God bought you with a high price. So you must honor God with your body."

Well, how do we honor God with our body if we trash His temple? If we're exhausted all the time or sick all the time, how do we have the energy to serve Him? If He has called us to be of a sound mind, to have a good attitude, and to be used by Him, we obviously have to be healthy in order to do that. So often we don't take responsibility for our health. It's much easier to say, "No. Food is the one acceptable sin in the church. God, when it comes to the refrigerator, don't talk to me."

But I want to ask you a few questions. How is your relationship with your refrigerator? How's it going? Good? Too well? Nurturing that baby?

I can relate to that all too well because I used to have a love affair with food. My definition of cutting calories was basically, "Stop licking the plate." For me, P.M.S. meant "Pass More Sugar." I was obsessed with food. I needed it when I needed it. When I was hungry, my personality changed from Dr. Jekyll to Mr. Hyde.

I remember one time when we had a family barbecue. I had run outside with my hamburger, French fries, and all my tasty junk food, and I had forgotten the ketchup. I was so obsessed with getting the ketchup that I ran through the screen door. I didn't notice that there was a door there because I was so focused on the food. If I'd given God even a quarter of the focus that I gave to what I was going to eat, we'd really have had a great relationship going.

I've come up with three reasons why not to eat healthy. First, we need to support the companies that make control-top panty-hose. Second, the chocolate industry would go broke. And third, what would I talk about if I didn't feel sick, tired, and bloated?

Have you ever thought about the great things that await us in heaven—spending eternity with the King of kings, seeing the crystal sea, having no more sickness, no more tears, no more death? Heaven sounds unbelievable to me. But I do have one question about heaven: Why is chocolate not mentioned in the Bible? I've looked for it over and over, and I've thought, "Maybe I just have the wrong translation." I can't imagine going to heaven and hanging out with my girlfriends by the crystal sea without chocolate. But I have since realized that the reason there's no chocolate in heaven is because when we get to heaven, we won't have P.M.S.

Exhaustion and bloating bonds us. "How are you feeling?" we ask our friends. "Tired? Sick? Bloated?" Talking about our health is a special bonding between us women. We're mad at people that feel good. I read a bumper sticker that said, "Lord, if I can't be thin, make all my friends fat."

The truth is, no one feels good when exhausted. Don't we always say, "I wish I had more energy"? We fall into bed at night so exhausted we can hardly see straight. We don't respect our body's need for rest. We don't respect our body's need for highly nutritious food. We refuse to exercise. And then we go to God and say, "Please, God, heal my body. Your Word says that I am healed."

I've never heard anyone say, "What can I eat to exhaust my body today? Boy, I hope what I ate these last two weeks makes me sick when I'm older." We spend billions of dollars every year in America alone trying to regain our health and energy. Think about the markets that would go broke if we started eating healthy foods.

IDOL-FREE FOOD

I want to ask you two questions. One: Do you think you have enough energy for your relationship with God, for your loved ones, and for the things that you personally want to accomplish in your life? Can you honestly say, "Yes, I have enough energy to do all the things that I would like to do and that God wants me to do"? Two: Are you suffering from poor health?

A recent survey was done in a Christian magazine that said that 90 percent of all prayer requests were for physical healing. Does that mean 10 percent of the church is healthy? If that's true, we're in trouble. Seventy-five percent of Americans are overweight. One in three Americans will develop cancer in his or her lifetime, according to the American Cancer Society. One million will die of heart disease this year, according to the American Heart Society. And millions more are suffering from chronic fatigue.

Does what we eat have anything to do with these statistics? I certainly didn't used to think so. I've always been one of those people who travel through life either in park or fifth gear. I was more consumed with my weight than nutrition. I didn't care what I put in my body so long as I could be thin. I was hung up on fat-free, sugar-free, chemical foods. I would have eaten cardboard if they'd put some artificial sweetener on it and told me it would burn fat. I was consumed with my weight for the wrong reasons. I didn't care about taking care of God's temple. I cared about worshiping my idol, which was my body.

One day I was speaking in front of a group of teenagers and their moms about entering into spiritual excellence, when all of a sudden my lights went out. As I was talking, I could feel myself getting weaker, but I ignored it. God had to get my attention. I fell over on the floor and was taken to the hospital.

The doctor did a lot of blood work and later came back to me and said, "You have been diagnosed with Epstein-Barr virus, which is basically chronic fatigue syndrome. It's a virus that breaks down your immune system and comes from ignoring your body's need for rest, restoration, and good nutrition." In other words, the doctor was telling me, "You're going to have to pull your lifestyle out of fifth gear and put it in park."

I was very discouraged. Up to that point, I had been able to overcome every obstacle in my life. God had freed me from a drug addiction and a food addiction. I had been able to keep my weight down. He had restored a family to me. I had been able to hurdle every obstacle that had hindered my relationship with the Lord. So I thought, *God's going to heal me. There is no problem. Because with God, all things are possible. All I have to do is pray. All I have to do is call all the prayer lines, and I'm going to be healed. End of story.*

I had every Christian I knew praying and asking God to heal me. I had to start canceling bookings. My little boy at the time was only four. I couldn't even get out of bed to play with him. I could not go to church. Whenever I would try to get up, I would get sick. I couldn't be up for more than twenty minutes at a time.

I thought I had done something wrong and that God was punishing me for it. Or I thought this was His way of saying, "You're done. The ministry is over. Go to bed." All I could think about was someone else raising my little boy. I was afraid that all he would remember about me was that his mom was always too exhausted to get up and play with him. I prayed for God to show me what it was I needed to get right in my life for Him to heal me because I thought I was dealing with sin.

I realized later that I *was* dealing with sin, an acceptable sin in the church. It was the sin of trashing God's temple and not presenting my body to God as a holy sacrifice. I began praying and looking up everything that the Bible had to say about food. I wanted to know what the Lord had to say about what I was eating and about healing. I was tired of the world's way.

God showed me through His Word how to restore my health and my energy. Since I have applied biblical principles to my eating habits, I have been able to enjoy my family and my son. God restored me back to health when I got serious with Him. When I decided that I no longer wanted to conform to the world but conform to Him, my body began working the way He designed it to.

I also had to give up dieting to be whatever size it was that I wanted to be that week. Have you noticed that we'll get healthy and lose weight and take care of ourselves for our high school reunion, but we won't do it for our family or for God? We'll put our efforts into everything for our own benefit, but have we ever thought of actually really offering our bodies as a sacrifice unto the Lord and sacrificing (giving up) foods that trash His temple?

Here are seven steps to success that I used to restore my health and energy.

Heavenly Way #1:
Listen to the Lifeguard—Your Body's Voice

God put a voice inside of your body to tell you when you're not well. If what you're eating isn't making you feel well, you know it. You know if you're getting in bed exhausted every night. I was sick because I conformed to the marketing magic of this world. I didn't want to die to my flesh. Food was not only a comfort to me, it was keeping me thin. I didn't care that it was artificial.

Unfortunately, millions of people are suffering from lack of knowledge. We know we don't feel well. Our bodies are talking to us, but we're not listening. We shut our bodies up by putting drugs in them, trying to drug ourselves back to health again. By ignoring our bodies' cry for rest, we pump ourselves up with anything we can to keep ourselves going through the day. As a result, corporate America makes billions of dollars off of our ignorance.

Yet your body, God's temple, is screaming, "Headache! Exhaustion! Indigestion! Bloating!" If you ignore it, what happens next? Disease sets in, and then you go to God and say, "Why me, God? Why me?"

In the Bible, sickness is only mentioned in connection with God's glory, unrepented sin, or defiling God's temple. Those were the three reasons for sickness. There are times when sickness is for the glory of God (Matthew 11:5, John 9:3, 11:4, Acts 4:21). But if you are not doing your best to take care of God's temple, and you're ignoring your body's cry, then you're going to suffer the consequences. That's *not* sickness for God's glory.

Listen to the lifeguard—your body's voice. What is your body saying to you?

HEAVENLY WAY #2: GO TO GOD

Once we've decided we're going to listen to our bodies, we need to go to God. Romans 12:1a (NIV) says, "Therefore, I urge you, brothers, in view of God's mercy, to offer your bodies as living sacrifices, holy and pleasing to God—this is your spiritual act of worship."

Our lives are like a tricycle. The big wheel in the front is the wheel that's driving us through life—the spiritual wheel. The two small wheels in the back are the wheels that put balance in our lives. One is our emotions, and the other is our physical bodies.

God made us mind, body, and spirit. He created us in His image. Our image is important to Him because what we are is the image of Christ to the world. Our act of worship is to take care of His temple, our bodies, by eating God's way.

Jesus said His nourishment came from doing the will of God (John 4:34). What is the will of God? And how can we do His work if we're exhausted? Most of the time we are so exhausted going from one place to the next the last thing we're thinking about is the will of God. We're thinking about our will to go to bed.

Are you too tired to do what God has called you to do? Go to God.

HEAVENLY WAY #3: EAT FOR THE RIGHT REASONS

The third step to success is to eat for the right reasons. Ask yourself, why am I trying to eat healthily? Is it so you can be the most beautiful person in the world? Is it so you can fit into a size 4? Your motivation to eat right should never be about your weight. It should be about your health and knowing that God has a call on your life.

First Corinthians 3:16–17 gives the right reasons to eat healthily:

> Don't you realize that all of you together are the
> temple of God and that the Spirit of God lives in

you? God will bring ruin upon anyone who
ruins this temple. For God's temple is holy, and
you Christians are that temple.

It's hard to comprehend what it means to be a temple where
God chooses to dwell. It may not seem that significant to us
because we don't think about a temple as anything great in this
day and age. But when this Scripture was written, the temple was
the lifeblood of the church. It was holy and artistic. It was the
most beautiful building anyone had ever seen.

Our bodies are the lifeblood of the church. He wants to use
our bodies to accomplish His mission. Back then, His chosen
place of dwelling was the temple. Today, it is in you and me. Is He
pleased when we trash His temple? We can't come to Him and
say, "God, heal me, no matter what I put in Your temple," any
more than we can drink a quart of alcohol and say, "Please pray
for me not to feel drunk."

The thing we need to ask ourselves is this: Is it worth the sacrifice to give up the foods that satisfy our cravings in order to conform to God's ways and our bodies' needs? It really is a matter of
choice.

Daniel thought it was worth it, and God blessed him. Daniel
didn't eat healthy food because he wanted to be the most buff
man of his day. That was not his focus. He didn't eat healthy food
because he wanted to be popular with the women. No, he ate
healthy to honor God with his body. He refused the delicacies of
his day and said, "I will eat God's diet." God blessed him as a
result with extra strength, extra wisdom, and good health.

That's the blessing, but that shouldn't be the motive. We should be motivated out of a desire to honor God with our bodies. One of my favorite verses is Ecclesiastes 10:17a. "Happy is the land whose king is a nobleman and whose leaders feast only to gain strength for their work." Write this one down and put it on your refrigerator.

God gave us food to live. He doesn't want us to live for food. He wants us to use that food to nourish and flourish our bodies. And the wonderful thing is, it tastes great, too, if it's prepared the right way.

HEAVENLY WAY #4: EAT THE RIGHT WAY

Does God care what we eat? If you take Proverbs 23:2–3 seriously, you would agree that He does. "If you are a big eater, put a knife to your throat, and don't desire all the delicacies—deception may be involved." God does care what we eat. The devil comes to kill, steal, and destroy. Who do you think he wants to kill, steal, and destroy? Us. And as long as we make God's temple our trash can, he can accomplish his mission one meal at a time.

God prepared a table for His children, but many times we refuse to eat from it. In Genesis 1:29, God says, "Look! I have given you the seed-bearing plants throughout the earth and all the fruit trees for your food." Every scientific study I'm aware of done in the last thirty years about recovering from poor health supports the conclusion that God's diet in Genesis 1:29 is the right road to recovery. We had it in the Word of God all these years. When we eat from the King's table, we feel great. When we eat raw food, live food—it makes us come alive. When we eat dead food, we feel exhausted.

I hear people say, "Hey, guess what? I ate a salad today!" They can't wait to tell you that one meal they mastered and conquered. It's a great feeling when you go to bed at night and know that you stuck to a godly diet that day. God rewards you with extra strength and wisdom if you've nourished His temple. You'll also have a good attitude because you'll feel better about yourself as you follow God's will. Believe it or not, deep down inside, every person craves excellent health. Even more than chocolate.

In my cookbook, *Eating for Excellence*, there are over one hundred recipes that will help you prepare God's food. I would like to share just a few key ideas from the cookbook that have helped improve my health.

Water is a key to good health. Water is something we don't think about enough, yet we can't live without it for more than four days. Water brings oxygen to our blood. It flushes out our systems, cleaning impurities out of our blood.

First thing in the morning, I get up and drink two huge glasses of water. The oxygen that it brings to my blood helps me wake up. Now, it may not be as tasty as your coffee, but it certainly is going to be a tasty treat to your body.

Second, artificial food is a key to poor health. Read the ingredients of what you eat. Commit to at least reading the ingredients before you eat them and find out what it is that you're eating. If you need a dictionary for what's on the packaging, put that food back.

Third, sugar is a drug. If you don't believe me, try to quit for a day. Try to go one day, two days. You literally go through with-drawals just like a drug addict does. You just can't help but think about it. You have to have it—until it gets out of your system.

Recently a study was done in a mental hospital that showed drastic results. The doctors changed the diet of the patients and took them off all white sugar and all white flour. Eighty percent of the patients completely recovered from their mental illness. How many women are running around right now feeling completely out of control, exhausted, depressed, overwhelmed, anxious, sick, and drained?

I challenge you: If your lifeguard is speaking to you, take some of these principles and apply them to your life. Get off arti-ficial food, white sugar, and white flour. See if two weeks from now your body doesn't speak a different message to you.

HEAVENLY WAY #5: EXERCISE FOR ENERGY

> Remember that in a race everyone runs, but only one person gets the prize. You also must run in such a way that you will win. All athletes practice strict self-control. They do it to win a prize that will fade away, but we do it for an eter-nal prize. (1 Corinthians 9:24–25)

I no longer exercise so my body will look a certain way. Because if my body doesn't look the way I want it to after I exercise, I get discouraged and stop exercising.

Our bodies are what they are. We can do our best and let God do the rest. We're not going to be perfect in every area of our life physically. We don't need to try to look like an anorexic, air-brushed model on the cover of some magazine. That's not the goal of exercise. I exercise because I love to go for walks and pray. It gets me away from the telephone. It gives me enough energy for my little boy in the morning. It relieves stress. It supplies oxygen to my blood.

We can live forty days without food—some of us probably wish we would—and four days without water, but we can only live four minutes without air. Our bodies need oxygen so badly. Oxygen is essential to life. It started back in the beginning of time when God blew a breath of life right up Adam's nose. It was oxygen that brought him to life.

Exercise can be a fun thing as long as it's not done excessively or for the wrong reasons. When I visit with a girlfriend, I'll say, "Do you want to go for a walk?" I commit to exercising fifteen to twenty minutes a day, whether it's walking with a friend or working out on exercise equipment at home. If you think about it, you could dance to your favorite Christian music for fifteen to twenty minutes a day. You could stand there while you're brushing your teeth and lift your elbows up and down for ten of it and have really white teeth and get rid of gum disease, too.

There are a lot of things you can do to be creative. You can go hiking with your children. You can commit to a girlfriend to go to the gym together a few times a week. Why should we take our stress out on others when we can take it out on an exercise machine?

God created us to be active. The reason the Word of God doesn't address exercise very much is that back in Bible times they didn't have remote controls. They didn't have cars. Everybody walked everywhere. There was no need to address that issue. But today, we have computers and remote controls, and we drive everywhere. We could park fifteen minutes from where we work and walk. There are so many alternatives.

Exercise detoxifies the blood, strengthens the heart, relieves stress, burns fat, helps depression, rejuvenates unhealthy cells, gives you energy, slows down the aging process, and strengthens your immune system. But aside from that, there's no need to exercise.

Heavenly Way #6: Relax and Restore Yourself

Success step number 6 is a big one—a difficult one for us women. Relax and restore yourself. I have called my husband from home while my son is still in school and said, "I am so tired."

"Why don't you lie down?"

"Oh yeah. What a concept! Ten minutes. Might get a catnap."

Don't you just love it when men have their practical answers? We just want them to feel it, not fix it.

> On the seventh day, having finished his task, God rested from all his work. And God blessed the seventh day and declared it holy, because it was the day when he rested from his work of creation. (Genesis 2:2–3)

God expects us to rest. Many of us take Sunday as a day to catch up on all the things that we overcommitted to that we didn't get done during the week. And we wonder why we start out Monday completely exhausted. We do not allow ourselves time to rest and relax. Then you know what happens? We pump ourselves up with artificial stimulants. We reach for one more cup of coffee, one more Coke, one more Snickers bar, just trying to make it through the day. Then we wonder why our bodies say, "I'm exhausted."

We need to rest. Matthew 11:28 says, "Come to me, all of you who are weary and carry heavy burdens, and I will give you rest." God expects us to rest. It only takes a few minutes to lie down for a catnap. Most adults, however, are worse than two-year-olds when it comes to taking a nap. We tell our two-year-olds, "Lie down. You're going to be tired." But they ought to be telling us, "Lie down, Mom. You're tired." They have the energy; we're the ones who need to rest. They should be putting us down for bedtime at eight o'clock and putting us down for naps.

Get the rest your body needs.

Another way to rest is to trust God with your circumstances and rest in Him. Worry can cause all kinds of health problems. Remember He is God! He is in control.

Heavenly Way #7: Eat and Enjoy

I have found a Scripture that I really enjoy because I love people, I love food, and I love to have those things together. It's a word from the wisest man who ever lived, King Solomon.

> So I recommend having fun, because there is
> nothing better for people to do in this world than

to eat, drink, and enjoy life. That way they will experience some happiness along with all the hard work God gives them. (Ecclesiastes 8:15)

This is not about what you can't have. This is not about denial. It's about desire. There are excellent ways to prepare God's delicious food. It can become a fun and enjoyable experience. God wants you to enjoy the food that He has prepared for you. The King has prepared a table. He wants you to dine with Him. Eat and enjoy.

SUMMARY

I pray that these steps will bless and encourage you. This message is not to put you in bondage to any type of diet. It's to set you free from exhaustion so you can be all God created you to be.

Take a few moments to think about some of the foods that could be edited out of your kitchen and out of your life that would restore your body to good health. May God bless you as you seek Him in what you should do regarding food and taking care of God's temple as you eat for excellence.

STUDY WORK

1. Memorize Ecclesiastes 10:17—"Happy is the land whose king is a nobleman and whose leaders feast only to gain strength for their work."

2. Write down your prayer requests. Take a moment to pray about these.

3. List some ways your body is talking to you: exhaustion, headaches, allergies, puffiness, skin problems.

4. List some ways you can honor God with your body.

5. List some good reasons for eating healthily.

6. What foods or drinks will you sacrifice to obey your body's cry and God's will for you to experience good health?

7. List some ways exercise has benefited you in the past or now.

8. What exercise are you going to do to build a better you? How many times a week? Commit it to prayer.

9. Define what rest and restoration is to you.

10. Name some healthy foods you enjoy eating.

Remember:

1. Listen to the lifeguard, your body's "voice."
2. Go to God.
3. Eat for the right reasons.
4. Eat the right way.
5. Exercise for energy.
6. Relax and restore yourself.
7. Eat and enjoy life.

5

You Are Not What You Weigh

Seven Solutions to Break out of the Barbie Bondage

Note: This chapter is by Lisa Bevere, author of *Out of Control and Loving It* (Creation House). In her new book, *You Are Not What You Weigh* (Creation), Lisa teaches seven solutions to break free from "Barbie bondage." She graciously agreed to share those solutions here. Her book will bless you tremendously.

SOLUTION #1: REALIZE THAT THE IMAGE IS A LIE

The first step in breaking free from Barbie bondage is to realize that the Barbie image is a lie. We must decide if we are going to embrace lies or embrace truth.

Jesus is the express image of truth. Even though there is no visual picture, no photograph of Him, we have been given the ability to know Him by the Spirit and through His Word. We are able to actually know Him intimately because He speaks to us in the secret place.

However, we often don't listen to the "still, small voice" that speaks truth and freedom. What we do listen to is the loud, blatant message that tells us lies and condemns the image that God has designed uniquely for us. Here is a passage from my book, *You Are Not What You Weigh:*

THE IMAGE OF THE LIE

If Jesus is the express image of the truth, then what is the express image of the lie? Just as truth needs an image for expression, power, and validation, so the lie must have an image, or it remains powerless.

Actually, we are made painfully and constantly aware of this image of the lie. It is everywhere we even happen to glance. It is projected on television and at the movies, on billboards, and splashed across magazine covers and assorted catalogs. Most of us encounter it daily on one level or another. It is the image built by multitudes of advertising and media experts who feed off our cultural external influences. It is the image of this present culture's ideal woman. In her *self,* she is nothing; it is what she *represents* that endangers us.

There are multiple portraits of her. She is presented to all ethnic groups. She is a woman, perfectly at ease with her self. She moves freely in any setting. She is adored by men and envied by women. All other women are harshly and unfavorably compared with this nameless woman. She never ages; behind her facade of perfection she mocks and makes note of every flaw and imperfection of others.

Her skin is flawless in tone and complexion. Her nose is straight—not too small or too large. Her eyes are bright and lack any dark shadows, circles, or lines around them. They are encased in luminous, wrinkle-free skin. Her lips are full and artfully shaped. Her teeth are perfect and gleaming white. Her hair is whatever ours is not.

Her body is perfectly proportioned and sits atop long, strong legs. Her breasts never age (or nurse)! All too often they are not even real. She is either taller or shorter than us—the perfect height!

This image is never what we are and is always just beyond our reach, taunting us with her seductive eyes. Who is she anyway?

Her name doesn't really matter; she is not real. She is an image molded and forged by the spirit of this world. What she doesn't have, plastic surgery readily supplies. Even this computer generation will not tolerate any imperfection in her—it reduces her thighs and cinches her waist while sweeping away any sign of imperfection in her skin. She is a deaf, dumb, and blind idol.

Though we know she is not real, young girls

and older women look at her in awe. The young are inspired, and the older are depressed.

Why would someone we have never met be able to influence us so profoundly? Because we have not allowed the imprint of God to influence us as deeply as she has influenced us. Without a definitive rousing of *His* standard, we have accepted the seductive, graven image of the world.

In Isaiah 44:9 it says, "The fashioners of an image, all of them are emptiness. And the things that they delight in cannot profit" (RHM). Our media and advertising people have "fashioned" this image for us. My paraphrase of Isaiah 44:9 in today's terms is this: "The modeled or fashioned image, all of them are empty and lifeless. What they value and prize cannot profit or help you." Isaiah tells us why this is so: "Their idols can neither see nor know." No wonder those who worship them will be put to shame.

The ancient idols or graven images were carved by men. They were overlaid with jewels and precious stones or metals. But no matter how much they were dressed up on the outside, they were still lifeless and dead on the inside.

I became a Christian when I was twenty-one. Looking back, I realize that when I looked the best, I was the stupidest. I was the most shallow and the most carnal. I was lifeless on the inside, so I tried to dress myself up on the outside. These images created by our culture are also lifeless. They have no life in them, and those who trust in them will find that they will reproduce death in their lives.

When we think about bowing down and worshiping idols as people did in the Old Testament, we think, "Well, I'd never do that." It all seems kind of silly. However, the images that you have before you, the images that you place around you, those are the idols and the images you become—not outwardly, but inwardly. Because what you keep in front of you, what you look at, what you try to emulate, is what you will become inwardly. It has to affect you. It does make an impact on you.

When we humans look at the created things instead of the Creator, we are turned over to the baser part of our nature. Idol worship is also present in the New Testament.

> Yes, they knew God, but they wouldn't worship him as God or even give him thanks. And they began to think up foolish ideas of what God was like. The result was that their minds became dark and confused. (Romans 1:21)

Our culture knows there is a God. If you ask anybody, they know there is a Creator. But they refuse to thank Him. They refuse to glorify or even acknowledge Him. As a result, their reasoning and their mentality becomes darkened. The image that is in front of them is what they actually become.

> Claiming to be wise, they became utter fools instead. And instead of worshiping the glorious, ever-living God, they worshiped idols made to look like mere people, or birds and animals and snakes. (vv. 22–23)

Because people desired to worship man rather than the Creator, God gave them what they wanted.

> So God let them go ahead and do whatever shameful things their hearts desired. As a result, they did vile and degrading things with each other's bodies. Instead of believing what they knew was the truth about God, they deliberately chose to believe lies. So they worshiped the things God made but not the Creator himself, who is to be praised forever. Amen. (vv. 24–25)

When we work to serve the works of our hands and the works of our flesh, God turns us over to be mastered by those desires and the lusts inside of us.

SOLUTION #2: TURN FROM SENSUALITY AND EMBRACE PURITY

I believe God is calling women to turn from sensuality and to embrace purity. We must turn from the sensual images the world gives and embrace God's image of woman. The goal of a fallen culture is to be sexually attractive. Therefore God has turned our culture over to be mastered by the desires that burn within it.

If we go on reading in Romans 1, we find that homosexuality follows closely behind sexual immorality (vv. 26–27). When we begin to call *evil* good and *good* evil, that is the sign of a nation under the judgment of God. When God turns us over to be mastered by ourselves and to have no restraint, He's actually saying,

"You don't want Me. I'll turn you over to fill your impassioned desires that burn within you."

On the cover of *Cosmopolitan* magazine you will always find the picture of the perfect woman. Listed on the cover are the articles that will make this perfect woman even sexier to whomever she wants to entice. The topics for one past month's subscription were: "Bedside Astrologer," "Is It the Real Thing, or Just a Fling?—Five Ways to Figure Out If It's Lasting Love Potential," "Sex Roles: Ten Things to Make Him Throb," "Four Sexiest Haircuts," "Men Confess: They Spill Out Their Secret Sex Sins That Every Guy Commits," "Hollywood Shocker," and "Fat-Burning Breakthrough Diet."

Almost every secular magazine for single women focuses on sex. *Glamour* magazine, which used to be pretty safe, recently listed the following article titles: "Doing It: Sex Do's and Don'ts—Do You Make Your Lover Feel Loved?" and "Escape from Birth-Control Hell." Women will buy this over and over again because our culture rewards the sexually attractive. Our culture says, "If you are sexually desirable, then you have worth. If you're not sexually desirable, you don't have worth."

Who are the people with worth in our culture? The young. The thin. The toned. The buff. And it keeps changing more and more. The standard is becoming stronger and stronger. The preachers of culture in our day present a seductive, glossy image that appeals to our flesh. They portray God's standard as narrow-minded and outdated.

So what *is* God's standard? How does He really measure us? Does He measure us by what is seen, or does He measure us by the unseen? First Samuel 16:7b (NIV) reveals God's perspective: "The LORD does not look at the things man looks at. Man looks at the outward appearance, but the LORD looks at the heart."

Turn from sensuality and embrace purity.

SOLUTION #3: EXCHANGE CONSCIOUSNESS OF SELF FOR CONSCIOUSNESS OF GOD

In the Garden of Eden, we find Adam and Eve both naked in front of each other and their God, and they were not ashamed. However, even back then the devil was up to his subtle tricks. He tempted them, just as he tempts us today, by taking their eyes off of the Lord and refocusing them on self. He told them they could be like God apart from God. He told them the same lies we hear today, "Don't serve God. Serve yourself. You can be your own god. You don't have to depend on God."

Adam and Eve exchanged the truth for a lie. As they sunk their teeth into that juicy, forbidden fruit, their eyes were opened, and they realized they were naked. Well, they had always been naked. But for the first time, they became self-conscious. They immediately attached shame and guilt to their nakedness. Why? Because anytime you exchange the truth for a lie, shame enters in.

I remember being young and feeling totally free from myself. My body served me. I climbed trees, swam, and played hard. And then when I was five, I lost my eye to cancer. I had to wear a patch on my eye for about three or four weeks that made me feel like I was one huge Band-Aid. In my kindergarten class, kids would make fun of me, calling me "Cyclops" or "One Eye"! All of a sudden, I felt like I was my eye. I wasn't myself anymore. I had become self-conscious.

Before Adam and Eve ate the fruit, they saw the eternal world rather than the physical world. They were God-conscious, not self-conscious. But as soon as their eyes were opened to evil, they were bound to the earthly, physical world and all that their senses could do for them. They ran from the presence of God to fulfill their self-focused desires.

I have heard people say, "If I could just feel good about myself, then I'd be happy." Well, I've learned something: To feel good about yourself, you have to be good. And no one is truly good except God (Luke 18:19). When Jesus was on this earth, people called Him, "Good teacher." Jesus did not answer them like this: "You know, I *am* good. And you can be good, too. Just follow Me." He said, "No one is good but God."

Jesus didn't come to make us feel good about ourselves. He came to reveal a good God. There's a big difference. One bases everything on our performance. The other bases everything on what's already been done for us. It's not about what I do. It's about what God's done for me. God wants us to break free from self-consciousness and become God-conscious. To do that, we must embrace some truths we have pushed aside.

SOLUTION #4: ESCAPE FROM THE IDOLATRY OF THE SCALE

The first truth you must accept is that you are not what you weigh. You must denounce the idolatry of the scale. The self-consciousness we feel about our weight is based on the image our culture worships.

I remember when I was fifteen coming in from school and my dad saying, "Come over here. Come here. Turn around. Oh, my gosh! You are getting so fat! Look at your bottom—it's huge! How much do you weigh?"

"I don't know what I weigh." At fifteen, I had only weighed at physicals.

"Oh, you're at least 140 pounds. You go back there and weigh yourself right now."

Well, he was right. At that time I was about 5'2" and a corn-fed heifer Indiana girl. I remember going into my room and stripping myself and looking at myself and thinking, "I'm disgusting! I'm gross! I'm horrible! I'm fat!"

I lost the weight. And when I did, everybody said, "Oh, you look great. You look wonderful. What have you been doing?" At fifteen, I thought, "You know what? When I'm thin, I deserve love. When I'm thin, I'm in control of myself. When I'm thin, I'm accepted. When I'm fat, I'm disgusting. When I'm fat, I don't deserve love. When I'm fat, I need to be rejected." And I began to measure myself by the way I weighed.

Now, it worked great for a while because Indiana girls have a certain level of thinness. Then I went to college in Arizona. California and Arizona girls were all a lot thinner and blonder than I was. I decided that I just wasn't thin enough.

There was always someone thinner or someone prettier—always. This realization sent me into a downward spiral. I became anorexic. It did not stop until I had been hospitalized for not being able to go to the bathroom for six weeks. I had abused laxatives and diuretics so badly that I had dehydrated myself and then began to poison my body.

I was afraid of eating. I was afraid of everything. The doctors and nurses thought I had some kind of horrible disease. They said, "We can't figure out how a twenty-one-year-old girl has the intestines of an eighty-year-old woman." I would just lie to them and say, "I don't know."

Then I became a Christian. I decided to stop drinking and partying. As a Christian, I was given permission to eat. Christians seemed to make food the highlight of every social event they had. I went from being an anorexic to being overweight.

I soon became engaged and bought a wedding gown that was a size ten. I went back home and became so depressed and so lonely that I outgrew my wedding gown. When I was lonely, I ate. When I was depressed, I ate. When I was happy, I ate. I ate because food tasted good, and it made me feel better—at least for a while.

I began to get mad about being overweight, so I cried out to the Lord, "Now, God, wait a minute. I don't understand this. I eat yogurt and an apple, and I can't lose weight. Or I eat everything in the whole refrigerator. I starve myself or indulge myself, but I can't be moderate. God, this isn't fair! I'm going to be married, and the first year I'm married I'm going to weigh 250 pounds because I'm going to have to eat three meals a day. I don't know what I'm going to do. You need to fix this problem."

And He said to my heart, "Lisa, your weight is an idol to you. It's what you draw your strength from, and it's what you give your strength to. If you will repent of this idolatry, I'll heal your body."

My weight and the food I ate were my idols. My perspective was warped by the cultural images that were so ingrained in my brain. At one time, I thought 83 pounds was the ideal weight for me. At 5'7", 83 pounds was not realistic. At that time, I weighed around 130 pounds.

God also said to me that day, "Lisa, I made you and I formed you. *I'm* going to tell you what you should weigh—not *Vogue*, not *Fit*, not *Shape*, not *Self.*"

God told me a figure, and I wrote it down and stuck it in my Bible. The figure was a lot bigger than I thought it should be, but it was smaller than what I was.

"Okay, God," I said. "I'll start dieting."

And God said: "No. You'll never diet again."

SOLUTION #5: STOP FOLLOWING THE DIET DEMONS OF THIS WORLD...EAT FOR EXCELLENCE

God surprised me when He said, "No. You'll never diet again." But I was even more shocked by what He said next.

"Lisa, I want you to go on a fast."

"Now wait a minute, God. You just told me not to diet and now You're telling me not to eat?"

"This is not about denying yourself food," He said in my heart. "This is a time for you, Lisa, to find out that I am enough to sustain you."

I remember thinking, "Wow! God, You're going to sustain me for the next three days?"

There's a difference between dieting and fasting. A diet will change the way you look, but a fast will change the way you live. A diet will change your appearance, but a fast will change the way you see everything for the rest of your life.

There are many ways to fast, but God specifically told me to drink only juice and water. I had so much sugar and salt in my body that needed to be flushed out of my system. I didn't think while I was drinking the juices that I was trying to lose weight, because the focus of fasting is being with God, not being without food.

God told me, "Take no thought as to what you're going to wear or what you're going to eat—don't worry about it. I'll take care of you. Don't even weigh yourself."

So I fasted for three days and didn't weigh myself afterwards. After the fast I said to myself, "Now I'm going to learn how to eat with moderation." The fast changed my appetite. I looked at food differently. It broke my habits.

A diet is a perverted fast. Satan wants all of us to think that a fast is just about food. But it's not. I am amazed that Christian women will diet, but they will not fast. I believe it is because Satan focuses our minds on the physical, and therefore, we do not embrace the spiritual.

Fasting does not only involve food. You can fast from magazines, telephones, or even television, which is my very favorite fast. Whenever you go on a fast, God sharpens you. You will find that the edge has returned to your life. God renews the way in which you look at the world. You become more spiritually-focused rather than worldly-focused.

For the next two or three weeks after the fast, I just ate until I was satisfied and then stopped. Before each meal I prayed, "God, this is from you. This is your provision for me, and I offer it with thanksgiving. I'm not going to worry if it's going to make me fat, thin—whatever. This is your provision. And, God, You'll perfect those things that concern me."

On my wedding day, God said, "You can get down your scale." I jumped on it, and I weighed the exact amount that I had written down on the piece of paper. For the past seventeen years I have weighed that amount, except for when I was pregnant.

SOLUTION #6: TEAR DOWN THE IMAGES IN YOUR HOME

When I pulled the *Victoria's Secret* catalog from the mailbox with the image of the seductive woman on the cover, I had a decision to make. With four little boys in my home, I had to think, "Is this something I want them to see? Besides that, should *I* be looking at these images?"

When God spoke to Israel, He would say, "Tear down the high places. Get all the images out." When the Israelites went to battle, God would deliver them for the sake of a righteous king. But if the high places and the images were not torn down, His protection was lifted. He gave them over to their false gods—"Let your idols save you!" (Isaiah 57:13).

God wants us to clean our homes of the idols and images that take our eyes off of Him. What magazines sit around your home? Do they promote God or self? Which television shows does your family watch? Do they teach God's values or the world's values?

I really don't want my children thinking that the only type of women that are attractive are a size 4 to 6. I don't have any daughters, but I remember being with my mother in the dressing room. To me, my mother was the most beautiful woman in the world. I would watch her try on clothes, and I'd say, "Mommy, you look so beautiful!"

She'd roll her eyes and say, "Oh, I look horrible in this! I look fat! Look at what this is doing to me!"

I remember thinking, "Wow! I can't wait to grow up and do that!" I will grow up and try on things and when someone tells me I look beautiful, I'll say, "I'm disgusting! I'm fat! I'm gross!"

I hear a lot of moms say, "I don't understand why my twelve-year-old daughter is worrying about dieting." Well, you know why? You may have never said anything to *her* about dieting, but she hears what you say about yourself. She hears what you say about other people. We must change the standard by which we measure ourselves and others. We must change the thinking of our generation and the next. It starts with you.

Get rid of the graven images in your home.

SOLUTION #7: BIND YOURSELF TO TRUTH

We must be people who will embrace the truth to a deeper degree than we've embraced the lie. Jesus said, "I am the way, the truth, and the life." Jesus is not a lie. He is the truth.

When I was a kid, I knew who Jesus was, but I didn't really know Him. I thought He was on the cross and was tired, so I didn't want to bother Him. I figured He was probably mad at me.

He wasn't a living Savior for me. I knew all the history about Him, but I didn't know Him personally.

There are a lot of people who may know me through my books and who may feel they can identify with me, but my husband knows me at a different level than anybody else. He knows my fears. He knows when I'm hurt or when I cry. I have a living, intimate relationship with my husband—maybe that's why we have four children.

The Lord wants to have that same kind of intimacy with you. He wants you to know the truth more than you've known the lie. Only truth can stop the progression of a lie. We must not let lies compete for our energy and our attention.

There are many women in the church who would like to *look* just like the world, but just not be part *of* the world. I believe it's time we raised a new standard. Proverbs 4:18 says, "The way of the righteous is like the first gleam of dawn, which shines ever brighter until the full light of day." The path of the righteous begins with a glimmer of light, but as you continue to behold Him and walk with Him, you are changed to be more like Him. His radiance becomes brighter in you. His beauty becomes your beauty.

But when I look at myself, I think, "I am nothing like God. I am the farthest thing from God." I remember the first time God told me I was not what I saw in the mirror. I had looked in the mirror and had seen a very tired, stressed-out mother of three children, pregnant with her fourth. I said, "My goodness! I look horrible!" And I was berating myself in the mirror over and over.

God said to my heart, "Lisa, you are not who you see."

"I am too what I see. I've earned the right to be stressed and tired. I know I'm tired, and I look tired."

"No. No. No. You are somebody no one sees. Lisa, the things that you measure yourself by, I don't see. I see you through the shed blood of Jesus. When I look at you, I see the sacrifice of my Son. I don't see brown hair. I don't see red lipstick. I see My Son. But I hear your heart."

The reflection in the mirror is not who you are. You are the person the Father sees when He looks at your heart.

SUMMARY (BY SHERI ROSE SHEPHERD)

It's freeing to know that we don't have to compare our image to images of this world. I challenge you to take the things out of your home that are causing you to engage in idol worship. There's no need for us to compare ourselves to an anorexic, airbrushed idol that's painted on the cover of some magazine. We were created in the image of God. That's the only image that we should be attempting to project to the world.

What images or idols in your home need to be removed?

STUDY WORK

1. Memorize Isaiah 44:9—"How foolish are those who manufacture idols to be their gods. These highly valued objects are really worthless. They themselves are witnesses that this is so, for their idols neither see nor know. No wonder those who worship them are put to shame."

2. Write down your prayer requests. Take a moment to pray about these.

3. At what point in your life did you become concerned about your physical appearance? What caused you to become aware of yourself? Was it a comment, photo, parent?

4. How have our culture's idols and images affected the way you see yourself?

5. List some ways you can turn from sensuality and embrace purity.

6. Describe how your weight affects how you feel about who you are as a person.

7. How have diets affected you mentally, physically, and spiritually?

8. When you look at magazines with airbrushed models, how do you feel about yourself?

9. Fast from looking at beauty magazines or images on TV for one week.

10. What image do you try to project to others?

11. How can we project God's image in us to the world?

Remember:

1. Realize the image is a lie.
2. Turn from sensuality and embrace purity.
3. Exchange an all-consuming consciousness of self for a consciousness of God.
4. Escape from the idolatry of the scale.

5. Stop following the diet demons of this world.... Eat for excellence.
6. Tear down the images in your home.
7. Bind yourself to truth.

6

Entering into Relational Excellence

Seven Things You Have to Be to Experience Excellent Relationships

So often we think about what other people need to be in order to make us happy. However, God tells us in His Word that there are seven things He wants us to be in order for us to experience excellence in our relationships.

One of the top-selling books in the Christian market today is entitled *Couldn't We Just Kill 'Em and Tell God They Died?* If a title like that can make it to the bestseller list, we must be having a little bit of trouble getting along.

It's easy when we're in relationships to say, "I would be a perfect wife if I had a different husband." It's always easier to blame the other person than to look at what we need to change.

I find myself being extra nice to people who are difficult, especially those who call themselves Christians. Eternity is a long time, so I'm hoping that if I'm extra nice to them here on earth, maybe their mansion will be on the other side of the crystal sea from mine.

Eternity *is* a long time, and we are going to be with each other forever. I believe God expects us to answer to Him for what *we* are doing, not what the other person is doing. The way we act toward others today will determine how those relationships turn out tomorrow.

Teddy Roosevelt said that the single most important ingredient in a formula of success is knowing how to get along with people. It's easy to love yourself, but it's pretty difficult to love people—especially those who are different from you. Since we can't change anyone but ourselves, let's focus on what we can do to build a foundation for excellent relationships.

RELATIONAL EXCELLENCE STEP #1:
BE WHAT YOU WANT OTHERS TO BE

People's attitudes toward you are very often a mirror of your own actions toward them. The Bible clearly says, "Try to live in peace with everyone" (Hebrews 12:14a), and "Do for others what you would like them to do for you" (Matthew 7:12a). The Golden Rule is God's standard. However, most of us don't quite apply it in all situations.

It's so easy for us to stand back when we're offended and react a certain way out of anger. But when someone's angry with us, we expect that person to be forgiving. Even though we haven't forgiven him or her for months, we expect better treatment. We will never experience excellent relationships that way.

When I learn to love someone in spite of her faults, in spite of her offenses, I become a friend. And then she becomes the friend that I want her to be to me, as well. The more I loved my mother and showed her affection, the sooner the walls began to break down in our relationship. I had to show her my respect even when she was not giving respect in return. Eventually we developed a wonderful relationship, which now exists today. The cliché "Kill them with kindness" really does work. Be unto others as you would have them be unto you.

RELATIONAL EXCELLENCE STEP #2: BE A BLESSING

The second step that we have to take is to be a blessing. There really is nothing more exciting than being a blessing to someone else. Proverbs 11:25b says, "Those who refresh others will themselves be refreshed." When you are a blessing to someone else, who really gets blessed? You.

It's so easy to be a witness in the world today and be a blessing. All you have to do is smile at someone in a stressful situation, and you've done something better than most of the world. Be kind. Be helpful.

Look for ways to help people. Ask God, "Lord, how can my life be a blessing today? How can I touch someone else's life?" Even if you're just patient with someone who needs a listening ear, sometimes that's enough. People need someone to listen to them. I physically hold on to listeners because I'm a talker. I don't let them go. That's why I'm an evangelist, not a counselor. I love to meet good listeners.

Be personal. Call people by name. You wouldn't believe how special it makes someone feel and how much of a blessing it is when you just call him or her by name. Make eye contact with people when you talk to them. Focus on them rather than the person just over their heads or to the right of them. Make them feel special by giving them all of your attention at that time.

There are so many little ways that we can be a blessing. I attended a church in Arizona with over ten thousand members. Yet the pastor went to the exit doors every Sunday to talk with anyone who needed him. The line would be a mile long, yet he never broke eye contact with whoever was right in front of him. That is being a blessing.

RELATIONAL EXCELLENCE STEP #3: BE A PEACEMAKER

Romans 12:18 (NASB) says, "If possible, so far as it depends on you, be at peace with all men." It doesn't say, "Depending on your circumstances or how well your day is going, be at peace with all men." Jesus said, "Blessed are the peacemakers" (Matthew 5:9a, NIV). He knows that you are going to have a richer life and a greater foundation for your relationships if you are at peace with all men.

How many of us are content with strife in our lives? When there is strife in our relationships, even if it's a distant relationship, it consumes our mind. Once there's anger, a fire bursts inside that burns us up from the inside out.

How can we be peacemakers? Create common ground. One of my gifts is "exhortation." For me, creating common ground is easy. If I don't have any, I come up with some. We can create common ground if we just look for it. Try to discover the other person's interests and listen.

Respect each other's differences. Did you know that God made us different by design? So why do we walk up to people and tell them that they should see things the way we do?

Right now, there's a great division in the church because we don't recognize we're different by design. If God created us differently, then it's okay to go to a church that has a different style than the church down the street. There's such a wall between Pentecostals and Baptists or Conservatives and Charismatics. No wonder the world doesn't want to come to our churches. They think, "How could they share anything with me? They can't even get along with each other."

We all worship differently. Some people feel comfortable sitting quietly and worshiping the Lord. Some of us like to do cartwheels and dance in the aisles. I'd rather have those people dancing in church and dancing before the Lord like David did than dancing in a bar. Who are we to judge those who want to make a joyful noise before the Lord? Who are we to judge those who want to worship the Lord quietly? God judges the heart. We need to create common ground. We need to respect each other's differences and do what we can do to be a peacemaker.

When we go out telling everybody how much better our church is than another church because we think ours is more biblical or spiritual, we're causing division. It's breaking God's heart and confusing the world about Christianity. We serve one God who has one Son, and if you know Him and live for Him, that's all that matters.

RELATIONAL EXCELLENCE STEP #4: BE QUIET

Learn to be quiet. Don't share people's private, personal experiences—whether you have just read about them or they have shared them with you. Even if someone shared an intimate experience with seven people including you at a luncheon, that's for her to share with others—not you.

We need to be careful and quiet. We don't need to climb on the ungodly gossip grapevine. What actually happens is we take personal information and gossip in the name of God. It sounds like this: "We need to pray for so and so, because blah, blah, blah, blah…" or "Oh, I know you're a prayer warrior, so I need to tell you every detail about this person's life."

Before we share information, we need to ask ourselves three questions. Why are we sharing this? Will it benefit the person that's hearing? And am I willing to let the hearer use my name as a point of reference?

Do you know what I do to people who share unnecessary information with me? I say, "Thanks for telling me that. I'll get the facts and see if you're right. Do you mind if I use your name as a point of reference?" You start saying that to people, and you will prune the gossip grapevine in the church very quickly. The second you want to use someone's name as a point of reference, you will hear, "Well, oh, I'm not really sure I heard that information accurately."

It's not godly to say, "Don't tell anybody this, but…" It breaks God's heart. He wants us to be quiet. He wants us to be trustworthy.

> *Those who refuse to slander others or harm their neighbors or speak evil of their friends.* Those who despise persistent sinners, and honor the faithful

followers of the LORD and keep their promises
even when it hurts. Those who do not charge
interest on the money they lend, and who refuse
to accept bribes to testify against the innocent.
Such people will stand firm forever. (Psalm
15:3–5, emphasis mine)

How many of us have caused division in our relationships
because we shared something we had no business sharing? Or
how many times has someone shared something about you that
devastated you and crumbled a relationship? We need to learn to
be quiet.

RELATIONAL EXCELLENCE STEP #5: BE FORGIVING

We need to give people the freedom to fail. There's not one who
is perfect except God Himself. Some people who are not forgiving
look for the perfect friend. They bond with someone and go
through a honeymoon period, but as soon as that friend fails,
they dump that person in search of a "better" person to befriend.
They leave a trail of tears behind them as they go from one friend
to the next—seeking that "perfect" relationship.

Everybody in your life is going to let you down at some time.
There's no way of getting around it. So, if you don't learn to be
forgiving, you're going to be a very lonely person in your later
days. Give others the freedom to fail. That's a great gift.

A very dear friend of mine came and stayed at my home. And
I'd have to say that she's the Martha Stewart of her time. I look up
to her because she is the greatest hostess. I was so nervous about

having her stay at my home. I was raised in a home where my mom worked from 3 to 11 P.M. There was no one home most of the time. Since we rarely had guests over, I was never given any lessons on etiquette and how to be a good hostess.

So this sophisticated, wonderful woman comes with her husband and stays at my home. I didn't even know that I was supposed to leave toilet paper out for her. I didn't have guest towels set out. I didn't have meals prepared. I was so nervous about it, and yet I didn't know what to do. No one had ever taken me through the steps of what you do when you have a guest. Yet, people expected me to be the perfect hostess.

I remember how precious she was when she came out of the bathroom the first day with no clean towels and no toilet paper. She said, "You know what we're going to do today? We're going to give you a lesson on exactly what to do when you have a guest over. And I'm going to write it out for you, so you're never put into a position that would make you feel embarrassed. I want you to know that I love you just for having me here. But I'm going to teach you what I have learned from my family."

I've become a great little hostess since that time because someone gave me the freedom to fail. She did not judge me but taught me what she had been blessed to know. I was so thankful that my friend imparted the very thing that she'd been blessed with, which was a mom and dad to teach her how to host others.

If there are people in your life who don't do things well like you do, don't judge them. Share the gift that you've been given and teach it to them. *Humbly*, with real love in your heart. Listen to Paul's advice:

> You, therefore, have no excuse, you who pass
> judgment on someone else, for at whatever
> point you judge the other, you are condemning
> yourself, because you who pass judgment do the
> same things. (Romans 2:1, NIV)

There is a big difference between *judgment* and *discernment.* *Judgment* criticizes; *discernment* cares. When you have a relationship problem, you need to go directly to that person and love him or her back to life again.

Galatians 6:1 says, "Dear friends, if another Christian is overcome by some sin, you who are godly should gently and humbly help that person back onto the right path." Why does God say "gently"? When we blow it, and we're saved, we know it. Do we need someone else to kick us while we're already down? No, we need someone to say, "You know what? I'm going to help you back up again. You're going to get through this. You're not going to fail. I'm going to stand beside you because I believe in you." That's what we really need from each other.

Scripture certainly doesn't say, "Give them disapproving looks, gossip about them at the dinner table, run from them at church, or pretend that you are perfect and they're not." That isn't what love is about. That isn't what a relationship is about. Relationships are about having the freedom to fail and about returning forgiveness to those who have failed you.

I have noticed that we are more forgiving with a perfect stranger in an elevator than we are with our own children and spouses. Do you know why we're willing to overlook the imperfections of strangers and acquaintances? Because we don't want to ruin the perfect, forgiving image of ourselves.

But when it comes to real relationships—our best friend, sister, brother, child, or spouse—why don't we extend that same grace to them? Is it because they already know the real us, and we don't care about that image? We can't fool them, so why bother. If we put as much effort into the relationships of those we love as we do into building a false image with others, we would have excellent relationships.

RELATIONAL EXCELLENCE STEP #6: BE LOVING

Shakespeare wrote, "Love all. Trust a few. Do wrong to none." Good advice, if you ask me. The only thing better than being loved is being loving. Many people are starving for love. They are so isolated by their own pain that they refuse to love anyone else, and they wonder why people don't love them.

The Golden Rule applies here as well: "Do unto others as you would have them do unto you." If you do not love, you're not going to receive love. There is one exception to that rule—God. He will love you even when you don't love Him. If we're Christians, to love or not to love is not the question. Christians can't choose whom to love, because He says that we're to love even our enemies.

First Corinthians 13:4–7 explains what love is. Love is patient. How patient are we, especially with those whom we say we love? Love is kind. Love is not jealous, boastful, proud, or rude. Paul says love keeps no record of when it's been wronged.

How many of us bring out the ledger of wrongs that have been done to us whenever a new one gets added? We need to let go of how we've been wronged. Love is never glad about injustice. It never gives up. It never loses faith. It's always hopeful. Love endures through every circumstance.

First Corinthians 13:13 says, "There are three things that will endure—faith, hope, and love—and the greatest of these is love." Remember, love will endure the longest.

John Maxwell says, "When it comes to handling yourself, use your head. When it comes to handling others, use your heart." A true friend is one that knows everything about you and loves you anyway. Have you ever had a friend like that? I've had a few in my life, and they have been a great blessing to me. Anybody can love when things are going great. What does that take? True character is when someone hangs in there with you even when things aren't going great.

A true friend of mine shared this poem with me:

A true friend knows my feelings.
An acquaintance only knows the facts about me.
A true friend reveals to me how she feels.
An acquaintance tells me about what she's done.
A true friend teaches me about myself.
An acquaintance tells me about others.
A true friend gives me freedom to fail.
An acquaintance will leave me when I let her down.
A true friend loves me for who I am.
An acquaintance loves me for what I can do.

Which one are you? If you are not applying these principles, you will not be a true friend.

RELATIONAL EXCELLENCE STEP #7:
BE IN LOVE WITH YOUR LORD

If you love the Lord, you can't help but love people. The seventh and most important principle is to be in love with your Lord with all your heart, mind, and soul. If you have an intimate relationship with God, you can't help but have more successful relationships with people, because you'll see things from God's eyes rather than through your own.

For me, loving my Lord absolutely has been the key to being able to love others. When someone offends me or hurts me, I go to God and say, "Lord, help me to love them." It's okay to go to God and say, "This person is difficult, Lord. I'm really battling. I feel anger. I feel jealousy. I feel like I'm coveting something that she has." We need to go to God for those things, so He can help us to have good relationships with other people.

It's when we try to handle these relationship problems ourselves that we get into trouble. We are all going to have times when we envy someone else, or we just simply can't get along with someone. That's when we should go to God and say, "Lord, I'm battling with this. I love You, and I give it over to You. Please give me the strength to love that person."

I read a precious story in *Today's Christian Woman* about a mommy tucking her little girl in bed one night. The little girl asked, "Mommy, if Jesus is in my heart, how can I tell Him I love

Him? Do you think if I wrote it on a stick 'em note and ate it, He'd read it?"

Take a moment to think about the people who have accepted you just the way you are, in spite of you. Make a list of how many people have been a blessing to you. So many times we are so consumed with our own problems, that we don't even see the blessing of friends and what God has truly given us.

SUMMARY

I know from personal experience how difficult relationships can be. I didn't have many positive relationships in my life to learn from. I'm grateful to God that in His Word He tells us exactly how to have excellent relationships. Even if you didn't have a good father or mother as role models, you have a heavenly Father who has the answers to everything you need.

I pray that you will apply these principles and be what God created you to be in relationships. Remember, the only person you can change is yourself. Don't wait for circumstances or other people to change before you enter into relational excellence.

STUDY WORK

1. Memorize Romans 12:18 (NIV)—"If it is possible, as far as it depends on you, live at peace with everyone."

2. Write down your prayer requests. Take a moment to pray about these.

3. Write out the characteristics of an ideal friend and/or mate.

4. Are you these things for your friends and/or mate?

5. Write down some names of people who have been a blessing to you and write them a note this week.

6. Ask God to reveal to you areas in which you may have caused harm by not being a peacemaker. Then go make it right.

7. Ask God to reveal to you areas in which you have shared information that has harmed someone in some way. Ask God for forgiveness and, if necessary, go make reparations.

8. Whom do you need to forgive?

9. How can you show 1 Corinthians 13 kind of love?

10. Write a love letter to God.

Remember:

1. Be what you want others to be.
2. Be a blessing.
3. Be a peacemaker.
4. Be quiet.
5. Be forgiving.
6. Be loving.
7. Be in love with your Lord.

7

Spiritually Fit to Win

Seven Things You Gotta Get to Win

Eighteen years ago, I developed what eight million women in America have today: an eating disorder called bulimia nervosa. When I had bulimia, there wasn't a name for it. So how could the girl who looked like she had it all together go tell someone, "Guess what? Behind closed doors, I'm eating compulsively and throwing up my food six to eight times a day"? People would have thought I was crazy. They may have thought I needed a drug to try to fix my depression. Or maybe I was ungrateful. I thought no one could have been able to relate to that kind of behavior.

I was obsessed with trying to perfect myself and win the approval of others. There was always one more thing I needed to do: lose five more pounds, win one more beauty title, achieve one more accomplishment. I finally gave up. I couldn't fill the empty pages of my life. Even though from the outside it looked like I had accomplished much, on the inside there was no life—I was dying a secret death internally.

Because God is the author of our lives—and because He

wasn't writing my story—there was nothing more to write about.

You can only perfect yourself so much. When it's all about you, what's left? The greatest deliverance I have found is deliverance from ourselves. When it's not just about us, all of a sudden we begin to truly live life to the fullest. Because my life was about me, I chose to take my life.

I ordered some sleeping pills from my doctor, thinking I would take those and end it all. I remember sitting in a hotel room by myself, holding the sleeping pills in my hand. I screamed at the top of my lungs, "God, do You exist? And if You do, show me!"

At that very moment God brought a memory back to me. There was a drug dealer who had sold me the LSD that had almost taken my life. He sold it to me on a Friday. That day a Christian reached out to this drug dealer and invited him to a church camp. Over the weekend, the drug dealer gave his life to Jesus Christ. He came back Monday and waited at his usual place. When we came to him to buy drugs, he handed us a Bible tract instead. He said, "Here's a spiritual high so great you'll never need these drugs again."

You cannot deny a changed life. Sitting there in that hotel room I wondered, *Could this God, this Jesus he was talking about, change my life as well?* I remember asking, "God, can You change my life and will You change my life?" Something inside of me made me put the pills away, and I fell asleep that night.

The next day a boyfriend of mine invited me to his grand-parents' house. His grandparents were missionaries from

Romania. And I want to tell you right now, if you're not saved and you have missionaries praying for you, *get saved*, because they'll wreck your life as you know it. James 5:16 says, "The earnest prayer of a righteous person has great power."

I started to see things differently as a result of their prayers. But what really changed me were their lives. They lived out the saying, "Preach Jesus always; use words when necessary." It's a godly life that changes a life. I desired to have what they had. I wanted their joy, contentment, peace, and purpose. I wanted their marriage. They were more alive in their seventies than any of my friends were in their twenties. They had something going that I didn't, and I couldn't buy it or decorate it or achieve it.

They asked me, "Sheri Rose, what do you want more than anything?" At the time, I wanted to be Miss U.S.A. I was pursuing a worldly crown. They said, "Let us tell you about the greatest crown of all. It's the crown of life appointed by God. An eternal crown can give you what you're looking for—a crown appointed by man cannot."

"How do I get this crown?" I asked.

"You need to receive Jesus as your personal Savior. It's a free gift. It's a free crown."

I thought to myself, *How can I possibly do this? I'm Jewish. My father said if I ever become a Christian I'd be disowned by our family.* I said, "I can't. I'm Jewish."

"Your Savior is Jewish, too," they said. "When you are ready, He is waiting."

I didn't become a Christian that day, but I didn't forget about it, either. What I love about God is you can call on His name anywhere. It doesn't matter where you've been. It doesn't matter what you've done. He desires to love you back to life again. He desires that you come to Him and have a personal relationship with Him. That peace won't come until your good ideas become God ideas, and your life is complete in Him.

Months later, I found myself in another hotel room once more holding a bottle of sleeping pills. The bulimia hadn't gone away. I was still trying to perfect myself. It still wasn't working. So once more I walked to the edge and looked over. Only this time, I called on the name of Jesus. I bowed down and received Him as my Savior. I said, "Jesus, if You are the truth, the way, and the life, if You are the true Messiah, come into my life like You did for that drug dealer, and change my life."

LIFE-WINNING KEY #1: GET A LIFE

The first thing you've got to get to win is a life—an eternal life. You have to have this kind of life to be spiritually fit to win. I can give you all these principles, but if you don't have a personal relationship with Jesus Christ, then you're not going to win. If you try to apply these principles without being empowered by the Holy Spirit of God, they're useless. All they are is positive thinking.

I heard a story about a famous artist who illustrated what the Christian life is all about. The artist had a son whom he loved and adored. The son had gone to war and had been killed. On Christmas Day a few years after the son's death, the son's best friend came to the father and said, "I drew a portrait of your son for you." Because he loved his son so much and was so devastated by his death, this portrait became more valuable to him than any of his nationally known artwork.

Soon after the artist passed away, an auction was held for his art. People came from all over the country to bid on them. The first piece held up was the drawing of the artist's son.

When the auctioneer said, "We need someone to bid on the drawing of his son," no one would bid.

The attendees said, "We want the valuable art."

And he said, "We must start the auction with the portrait of the son per the request of the artist, in order for us to auction off any of the other art pieces."

One man raised his hand because he realized that there must be some value in the portrait because the father valued the son. He said, "I'll start the auction with ten dollars."

No one else bid, except for this one man. The auctioneer handed the painting of the son to him and said, "The auction is over."

Everybody around said, "What? How can this be?"

And he said, "The man said in his will, he who gets my son, gets it all."

Just like the lucky man at the auction, he who gets the Son of God, gets it all. If you know the Lord and nothing good happens to you in your life—not one thing, not one worldly blessing—you still get it all, because you have eternal life. You're going to be in a place where there's no more sickness, no more tears, and no more death. You are going to live forever with the King of kings and the Lord of lords. You will celebrate in eternity. If you get the son, you get it all. Jesus says, "I am the resurrection and the life.

Those who believe in me, even though they die like everyone else, will live again" (John 11:25).

Get the Son. Get a life.

LIFE-WINNING KEY #2: GET A GRIP

When I won the crown of Mrs. United States, my little boy was in kindergarten. Show-and-tell is a big deal for kindergartners, so my son wanted to tell everyone his great news. He proudly raised his hand and stood up and said, "Everybody, my mommy is the new queen of the country."

Now, you have to understand that I am just an ordinary mom. On weekdays, I'm not particularly concerned about wearing my rhinestones, styling my hair, and doing my makeup. When I don't wear makeup, like most blondes, I don't have a face. The particular day that he'd announced that his mommy was the queen of the country, I had come to pick him up in gray sweats. I had just worked out, I had no makeup on, and my hair was in a bun.

His teacher walked him out to my car. "This is so cute," she said. "Your little boy loves you so much that he actually believes you're Mrs. America."

"I am."

She laughed.

You see, this woman expected me to look a certain way. She had an image in her mind of how I should appear. She must have imagined that I would pick him up in an evening gown or a swimsuit with my banner and crown on. She had preconceived notions that I didn't quite measure up to.

The truth is, if we are Christians, we do wear a crown. We wear an eternal crown and a banner that is love. We wear the name of Jesus Christ, and we have a reign while we're here on earth. We're not even citizens of this place. This isn't where we live. We are foreigners in this world according to the Word of God. We're just visiting. Since we are reigning here and representing Christ, we need to be aware of what we look like to others. It's sad when someone looks at us and says, "You're kidding! You're a Christian? Wow!"

Second Timothy 4:8 says we have a crown of righteousness. First Peter 5:4 says that crown is unfading. First Corinthians 9:25 says our crown is eternal. Revelation 3:11 urges us to hold on to what we have so that no one will take away our crown. And Proverbs 16:31 reminds us that gray hair is a crown of glory (even if we color it).

Get a grip on who you are. The Bible tells us as a man thinks in his heart, so is he (Proverbs 23:7a). If we do not see ourselves as a child of the King, if we don't recognize that God chose us to represent Him, we will get hung up on the things of the world, and we will not ever get a grip on who we are.

We are told by the world that we're suffering from a poor self-image. But I want to tell you that a poor self-image isn't the problem. The problem is we have an *inaccurate* self-image. We were created in the image of God. Self-images don't come any better than that. We are of a royal priesthood. First Peter 2:9a says, "But you are not like that, for you are a chosen people. You are a kingdom of priests, God's holy nation, his very own possession." You did not choose Him. He chose you to represent Him. The solution to our self-image problem is to see who we really are: royalty.

I remember I was in New York City with my husband, and we had been praying for some divine appointments that day. We spent some time with a pastor and his wife, but nothing else eventful had happened. At the end of the day, two young girls walked up to me, and they asked me if I was celebrity. I said, "I am. I'm a daughter of the King. My Father created the heavens and the earth."

"Excuse me. Exactly what are you talking about?"

I said, "Well, I received Jesus as my Savior and that makes me a daughter of the King."

"I don't get it. What do you mean, 'the daughter of the King'?"

"Do you believe in God?"

"Of course we believe in God. We're Jewish."

"When you receive His Son, you become a daughter of the King and a child of God. Because I've received His Son as my Savior, I am a daughter of the King."

"Well, we're Jewish."

"What a coincidence! So is my Savior, and so am I."

One of them said, "Well, I just got out of a drug rehab center. People like me don't go to church."

"Well," I said, "let me tell you a story."

I shared my testimony. Steve and the pastor and his wife shared Scriptures with them. One of the little girls, who had not spoken the whole time, started shaking. Tears poured down her face.

"Are you okay?" I asked.

"Are you, um, angels?"

"Far from it. But we shine like light in the darkness. This morning we asked God for divine appointments. He orchestrated this moment in the heavenlies, so we could lead you home and to eternity and so that you also could become a daughter of the King."

Being Jewish, I like the whole princess idea. I've always been called a Jewish-American princess because I was the only daughter. But to be a daughter of the most high King, there's no greater honor than that. I've had crowns appointed by man, but the greatest crown of all is the crown of life appointed by God. So I take this reign of representing Christ pretty seriously.

I pray that you would get a grip on who you are and take it seriously as well. God wants to use you in ways that you've never dreamed possible. If you do not recognize who you are in Christ, you will never be used by God because you'll be too consumed with an image that you're trying to project to others.

LIFE-WINNING KEY #3: GET READY FOR THE CALL

This is the toughest one. David got ready for his royal call in a cave, running for his life. Joseph got ready for his call sitting in a prison. Queen Esther got ready for her call growing up as an orphan. I have found that the royal call God has on our lives is not about comfort. It's about true character that glorifies Him.

Do you know how a silversmith gets his precious metal? He puts it into the fire and never takes his eyes off of it. He doesn't

SHERI ROSE SHEPHERD

remove it until he can see his own reflection in it.

Many of us are feeling the heat in our lives. We think, "God can never use me! There are too many fires going on in my life." But you don't know what God is doing. Instead of saying, "Why me?" Why don't we say, "Lord, what do I need to learn in this, so I can move forward with the call that You have on my life?"

God does have a call on your life. That's the truth. So when you're feeling the flames all around you, ask God, "How can I use this experience to glorify You? What can I learn from this hardship? How can I help someone else who is experiencing the same pain?"

When I became a Christian, I was on a salvation honeymoon. I would literally trip people to tell them about the Lord. I wanted the world to know the freedom in Christ.

But there came a time when I had to face some fears and some facts. My Jewish family wasn't saved. Even though I was willing to profess Jesus to the world, I wasn't willing to tell my Jewish family that I had been born again.

I remember sitting at a dinner with my father one night. "You're so different," he said. "Where have you gotten this joy? You seem so at peace with yourself."

"Dad," I said, "you know that Jesus who you told me wasn't the Messiah? Well...Dad, I was going to kill myself. I had the sleeping pills in my hand. But I called on the name of Jesus, and He gave me a new life and a new attitude."

Now, I'm a daddy's girl. I'm my father's only daughter. I know he liked that I had contentment and peace and direction. I know he praised God that I wasn't going to take my life and was glad God had touched my eating disorder. He was very grateful for the gift, but he missed out on the Giver of the gift for himself.

"You know what?" he said. "That's fine for you. Just don't tell your Jewish grandmother."

A few weeks later, I found out that my grandmother was dying. Well, I was raised with a mother who didn't show love in a language I could understand. My grandmother was the only woman who had ever shown me the kind of love that spoke to my heart. So you better believe I wanted my grandmother to go to heaven with me.

I went to the hospital with my best friend. I laid my body over my grandmother's and said, "Grandma, I want you to go to heaven with me."

She said, "I will."

"Grandma, you need Jesus."

She turned her back on me and said, "Get out of my room. You are the one that is dead in this family."

And I lost her. I learned that day that there is a price to pay if you want to finish your faith strong. The Bible says if you love your family more than you love God, then you really don't have the love of God in you. Because ultimately, He's your heavenly Father. And you are obligated to do what He wants you to do, even at the cost of losing your own life or a family member.

I was devastated. Needless to say, my salvation honeymoon ended. For two years, I had to learn to walk alone with the Lord. I began to understand what it meant to be adopted into the Kingdom of God. I understood there was a Holy Spirit who comforted me in those times, and there was a God who was strong when I was weak.

I also learned that God honors obedience. Two years later, I received a phone call from my family. My Jewish family had become born-again and had received Jesus Christ as their Savior! God is faithful when we are faithful (and even when we're not). We can trust Him when we go through a storm. His ways are the right ways.

There's always going to be a battle between the mind-set of mediocrity and the spirit of excellence. God has called us to the excellent way, which is not the easy road. It's the hard road, but it's the right road. It ends in winning, not in losing in life.

How do we get ready for the call? We get ready by obeying the Lord. He says, "If you love Me, you're going to obey Me." If we can't do what He needs us to do in the little things, how in the world can He use us to do the big things? He never will. He wants us to trust Him in the little things (Luke 16:10). We're never going to see abundance in our lives without obedience. We're not going to see finances without tithing. We're not going to have wisdom without the Word. We're not going to have victory without accountability.

In the thirtieth chapter of Deuteronomy, Moses warns God's people. Here's my paraphrase of that warning: "God wants to bless you. He wants to bless you even more than your forefathers, but your blessing is dependent on your obedience. If you don't obey the Lord, not only will you not see the blessings of God, but you will cause Him to lift His shield of protection off of you."

Satan gets too much credit for attacking Christians. If your finances are being attacked, is it Satan? Or are you just not tithing? If you are not having victory in your life, are you reading the Word? If you are involved in sinful activities, do you have someone to hold you accountable? Satan gets a lot of credit for our disobedience.

Not all of God's promises are unconditional, only His love is. He loves us without strings attached, but His blessings are dependent on our obedience. He tells us exactly how to obtain His blessings.

If you're melting in the flames right now, trust God. Ask Him what He wants to teach you, and get ready because a royal call is coming. He's going to start a fire inside of you, and He's going to take whatever pain you're going through right now to use it for His glory.

LIFE-WINNING KEY #4: GET AVAILABLE

I was on an airplane once when the pilot made an announcement. He said, "Folks, I'm going to have to make an emergency landing. We have a passenger on board who has had a stroke, and we need to get to the nearest hospital to save his life."

The businessman sitting next to me said impatiently, "I don't have time for someone to die. I have a business meeting to get to." I was sitting there burning with anger. I said, "Please, God, let me punch this man out, and I will apologize later."

But then the Lord showed me a reflection of myself. He said, "That's my children. Every day they sit next to someone who's dying, and they don't have enough time to give him a message that will save his soul for eternity. They're not available for me because they're too consumed with their destination of the day."

There are divine appointments everywhere we go. We can keep our divine appointments anywhere we are. It doesn't really matter. We can be standing in a grocery store line or taking a walk in the neighborhood. Our divine appointments don't have to be vocal. They can be a silent prayer. For those of us who are more vocal than others, we can give a word of encouragement. God gives us divine appointments. The Word of God says our steps are ordered by the Lord, if we're available.

One time I had been on the road and someone had given me a gift certificate to get an hour and a half massage. I was so excited! I thought, "Oh, this is going to be the best!" I couldn't believe it when my car broke down before I could get to the appointment. The masseuse said she wouldn't be able to give me another massage for two weeks if I didn't make my appointment.

A man walked up to help me with my car, and he said, "So, what do you do?"

I was in such a hurry to get my car fixed, I did not want to waste time on small talk. I said impatiently, "I don't want to talk about what I do right now."

"I'm just curious. I saw a book in the back of your car."

"Well, I'm a Christian speaker and a writer."

"Oh, well, I've been dating this Christian girl, and she's been trying to tell me I need Jesus in my life."

Then it hit me. "You're the reason I'm missing my massage."

I stopped and told him about the Lord and gave him one of my books. As soon as I was done sharing the gospel with him, the car started. Two weeks later I got a thank-you letter from his girlfriend because he had accepted Christ.

When God interrupts your day, you never know what He has in mind. You may be sitting in traffic because He wants you to spend an hour in prayer since you didn't spend five seconds in prayer before you walked out the door. You don't know what the Lord is orchestrating, but you do know that your steps are ordered by the Lord. You do know that every day you have a divine appointment. You do know that you're a child of God. He wants to use you to be light in darkness, and we're in darkness every day.

In the morning, ask God for divine appointments. He will give them to you when you ask—so watch out! Start praying for divine appointments for your kids and watch how God's hand moves. Your kids will get excited about their faith. If you're keeping your divine appointments, you will have more exciting things to talk about with your friends than gossip.

If you're not focused on eternity, you're only focused on yourself. If you're not available for God, then you're going to become a grumbler, whiner, and complainer because you're not going to be thinking about anybody but yourself.

I have learned that if the devil can't make you bad, he will make you busy. If he can keep you busy, he can keep you from making your divine appointments. And if you're too busy to be available for God, you're busier than God has ever asked you to be.

LIFE-WINNING KEY #5: GET EXCITED ABOUT THE CALL

I love what John Wesley says. "Get on fire for God, and people will come watch you burn." But God says something that's a little bit scarier and would motivate me more to get on fire for Him. Revelation 3:16 says, "But since you are like lukewarm water, I will spit you out of my mouth!" God desires complete commitment to Him, not complacency.

If we're not excited about the call that God has on our lives, if we're not excited about what God's doing in our lives, how in the world are we going to excite anybody else? We wonder why our kids don't want anything to do with our faith. We wonder why our neighbors don't want what we have. Is it because they don't see anything in our lives that they need?

LIFE-WINNING KEY #6: GET FAITH

What is faith? Hebrews 11:1 says exactly what faith is: "It is the confident assurance that what we hope for is going to happen. It is the evidence of things we cannot yet see."

I have to tell you that after my family got saved, I got pretty confident in my ability to pray. God's Word says if you delight yourself in Him, He's going to give you the desires of your heart (Psalm 37:4).

Well, I decided I wanted a husband. I didn't want to be single anymore, so I started praying for a husband. I thought I should probably help God out, and the only way I was going to find this Christian husband was to date every man I could ask out or who would ask me out. I was kind of "missionary dating," giving God a wide range of candidates to pick from.

I sort of accidentally got engaged to three men. It really was an accident. There's a chapter about them called "A Few Good

Men" in my book, *Life Is Not a Dress Rehearsal* (Broadman & Holman). So there I was, dating all these different men. Within one week, three different men proposed to me, each saying God had told him I was to be his wife. So I thought, "This is interesting. Maybe I can appeal to the Old Testament. Maybe because I'm Jewish, I get three husbands?"

I was in a corner. I didn't know which of the three was God's pick for me, and I was afraid of hurting anybody's feelings. So I took all the rings, and then for about a month I hid out. To my surprise, one day all three of them showed up at the same time. You can imagine how that story ended. The next chapter in my book is entitled "Three Wise Men" because they all left me.

I decided after that fiasco that I didn't need to help God out anymore. Maybe I could actually let Him be God. After waiting on Him for six weeks, I met Steve, the man who would become my husband. We've been married now eleven years, and we have a son, Jacob.

Steve was raised in a functional family. He's a functional man. Well, at least he was before he married me. But he needed to marry me because he had no stress in his life prior to that. And I think everybody deserves a little stress in his or her life.

He and I shared the same vision. Steve was a professional actor at the time. He had just done a movie, *Bill and Ted's Excellent Adventure.* I was producing modeling and acting showcases (a little like *Star Search*). We would bring in Hollywood casting directors and agents, and we would showcase models and actors.

It was somewhat of an "ambush" ministry. At the dress

rehearsal we would set up and do church and say to the models and actors, "Before you meet the agents, we want you to meet the Savior." Steve and I would share our testimonies, and we would actually have altar calls right there at rehearsal. We saw over 80 percent of these people come forward, either for prayer or to receive Christ, month after month.

As we were on the road with this ministry, I got pregnant and miscarried a baby. Jacob, our son, was four. When Jacob was five, I got pregnant again and miscarried that baby. I became very ill to the point that we could no longer run our production company. This was devastating because Steve and I loved what we did.

I remember thinking, "Why would God take two good people who love Him and want to serve Him and allow all these things to happen?" I started thinking, "Well, maybe it's because of the old sin in my life, and now I'm paying a great price." I didn't know what God was doing, but for whatever reason everything started to shut down. It was a horrible experience.

We ended up losing everything. We had to sell our home. Steve was out looking for a job, too, because we had owned the production company together. No doors seemed to be opening up for him. After the second miscarriage, I was diagnosed with chronic fatigue syndrome. Our world seemed to be falling apart.

What I didn't know was that God was shutting those doors because He had a different plan. He wanted us to go a different way.

Our production company used to run the Mrs. Arizona pageant. The winner of that pageant went on to compete for the Mrs. United States title. Because we had lost everything, and I was in such poor health, I called the director of the Mrs. United States pageant to tell her we would not be able to produce the Arizona pageant for them. I told her they would have to find a new director.

To my surprise, her response was, "No way! You're not leaving me without an Arizona representative. You have a contract with me. If you can't host the pageant, you're going to come to Las Vegas and stand in as Mrs. Arizona."

I said, "No, you don't understand. I'm twenty-three pounds overweight. I just miscarried two babies. I've got chronic fatigue syndrome. And we're about to file for bankruptcy." But she wouldn't budge.

There were many Christians in my life, including my pastor and his wife, who felt God was opening the door for me to go to this pageant. If God was giving me a way to go lead some people to the Lord, I was excited to do that. But I had no idea that He was going to use it to turn my life around.

Every person who knew me wanted me to go to this pageant. People donated money and clothes. A chiropractor gave me free adjustments. People worked with me with my chronic fatigue syndrome. I got free nutritional supplements. Every door opened for me to go to this pageant.

There's a moral to this story: If God is closing a door in your life, get your face out of the way and it won't hurt so badly.

It was faith that gave David the courage to stand before the giant. It was faith that saved Noah's family from the Flood. It was faith that gave Sarah and Abraham a baby. It was faith that brought down the walls of Jericho. It was faith that saved Daniel from a lion's den. It was faith that gave Elijah the power to make the rain stop. It was faith that gave Shadrach, Meshach, and Abednego the courage to get in the fire, trusting that God would rescue them. It is faith that moves the mountains in our lives. Jesus said that faith the size of a mustard seed will move a mountain (Matthew 17:20).

Faith is basically saying, "He is God; I am not." I believe Him, and I will do what He tells me to do. All God is saying to you is, "Trust me. Believe me. Have faith in me—because obviously, nothing else is working." I think it's funny that He tells us that it only takes faith the size of a mustard seed to move some mountains. He's not really asking a whole lot. He's just saying, "Could you just believe in Me a little bit and watch what I do? Because then your faith will increase, and I'll start moving some serious mountains in your life." It all starts with faith.

LIFE-WINNING KEY #7: GET TOUGH

To be spiritually fit to win, you're going to have to fight. You're going to have to fight your flesh to do what's right. You're going to have to fight the enemy, too, because you're on his hit list.

Paul shared with Timothy that righteousness for the sake of Christ is definitely worth fighting for:

> I have fought a good fight, I have finished the race, and I have remained faithful. And now the prize awaits me—the crown of righteousness that the Lord, the righteous Judge, will give me on that great day of his return. (2 Timothy 4:7–8a)

It's going to be a fight. There's no way of getting out of it. You'll have to fight to win the battles in your life.

Whenever something comes against me, it helps me to focus on eternity. If you haven't had something come against you, I can promise you right now, you will at some point in your life. You'll have to come to a point where you say, "You know what, Satan? No matter what you bring against me, I'm going to fight, and I'm going to finish my faith strong." If God doesn't change your circumstances, you need to be willing to say, "Even if He doesn't change a thing, I'm going to fight and finish my faith strong."

Rachel was thirteen when she was diagnosed with leukemia. She had been in one of our productions in the modeling and acting showcases. Her parents had asked me if I would call and encourage Rachel. To my surprise, when I called to encourage Rachel, she encouraged me.

When I called her, I was afraid of what I was going to say to her. What do you say to a thirteen-year-old who has leukemia? All I knew that I could say was that I would pray for God's healing for her. But in the back of my mind was the thought, "What if God doesn't heal her?"

Rachel's response was quite different from what I expected. She said, "Sheri, I don't know how much time I have left, so you know those divine appointments you were talking about? Can you pray that I'll have one every day before I go home to be with the Lord?"

Talk about a reaction. It's not how you act, but how you react. Rachel was saying to Satan, "Even if I don't get healed, I'm going to take as many people as I can home with me to the other side of eternity before I leave. Ha! Ha! Ha!"

You need to laugh in the devil's face and say, "I don't care if my marriage never gets fixed. I don't care if my husband never changes. I don't care if my child never comes back to the Lord. Guess what, Satan? I'm going to fight, and I'm going to win souls for Christ. I'm going to be what God called me to be. I'm going to win."

Rachel spent three years having divine appointments on her campus. It was very fun to talk to Rachel. Because of her cancer, the kids would say, "Why are you worried about me? You're the one that's dying." Her cancer actually gave her a voice in a secular high school that had a very high drug problem and gang problem. For three years, this precious princess went from junior high to high school, witnessing the gospel.

On her sixteenth birthday, she stood up in front of all of us and said, "I'm ready to go home to be with the Lord." How many sixteen-year-olds could stand up and say, "I've done what God's called me to do, and I'm ready to meet my Maker"? How many forty-year-olds could say that? She wrote a letter to her high school. And then she went home to be with the Lord. Her last request before she died was that her high school could come to her funeral, so her pastor could read the letter she had written.

Because Rachel had made such an impact on her high school, the principal made buses available. I had the privilege of attending that funeral, and I've never been the same since. My passion for divine appointments is because of a little thirteen-year-old with leukemia who was determined to keep hers.

Hundreds of kids that weren't saved, some of them still high when they were sitting there in the church, heard this letter:

> Dear Classmates, do not mourn for me. For today I am in paradise where there is no more sickness and no more tears. My only prayer is that I would see you someday on the other side of eternity. And my Savior, Jesus Christ, made a way for you to get there.

Then the pastor said, "How many of you want to know that when you die, you will be celebrating with Rachel in heaven on the other side of eternity?" Hundreds of kids walked to the front of the church and gave their lives to Jesus Christ.

SUMMARY

One little girl with leukemia who was determined to apply these seven principles to her spiritual life won hundreds of young people to the Lord. Who knows how many of those young kids are going to be pastors, evangelists, or teachers? How many of them are going to go back and win their families to Christ?

All because of one little girl who recognized who she was in Christ and realized that her citizenship wasn't here anyway. She decided that she was going to fight to the end, and she was going to bring as many people home with her as she possibly could.

Get fit to win.

STUDY WORK

1. Memorize 1 Peter 2:9—"But you are not like that, for you are a chosen people. You are a kingdom of priests, God's holy nation, his very own possession."

2. Write down your prayer requests. Take a moment to pray about these.

3. Write about your salvation experience. When, how, where—and how it has changed your life. If you don't know the Lord and want to have salvation, repeat this prayer to God: *Dear God, please forgive me for my sins. I believe Your Son Jesus died on the cross, was buried, and rose from the dead to give eternal life. I want to receive that free gift of salvation today. Thank You for writing my name in the Book of Life.* Date_____ Now go tell someone what you've done.

4. What are some things you want to change about yourself to bring glory to God?

5. How can you get ready for the call God has on your life?

6. What things might you remove from your schedule to make you more available to God?

7. Ask God for a divine appointment today.

8. What excites you about being a Christian?

9. Write about a time that you had to have faith and God proved Himself to you.

10. What do you need faith for now?

11. How do you want to be remembered when you're gone?

12. Honestly, is that how you would be remembered if you died today? If not, what can you do to leave the legacy you desire to leave?

Remember:

1. Get a life…an eternal life.
2. Get a grip on who you are.
3. Get ready for the call.
4. Get available for divine appointments.
5. Get excited about the call.
6. Get faith and obey.
7. Get tough and fight the good fight.

Conclusion

⟶⟵

My final challenge to you is this: Is it worth building a foundation of excellence in every area of your life so that you can impact people for eternity? The greatest inheritance we can leave behind us is a good example. What do you want to be remembered for at your funeral? What would you be remembered for if you died today?

I pray that you will take the tools that have been given to you in this book and build a foundation of excellence. And I pray that you will share with others how they can build a solid foundation, too.

When God pulls you out of something, He pulls you out so you can pull others out also. He wants to use what you've learned not only in your own life, but also in your loved ones' lives and in the world. I pray that you would keep your divine appointments and finish the fight.

I look forward to celebrating with you on the other side of eternity. I hope you've enjoyed our journey toward excellence.

I have a closing prayer for you from Psalm 20:4–5 (NIV):

May he give you the desire of your heart and make all your plans succeed. We will shout for joy when you are victorious and will lift up our banners in the name of our God. May the LORD grant all your requests.

May you be victorious as you build your foundation for excellence!

Please write or call for booking requests, media interviews or for more information on Sheri Rose's speaking schedule or any of her other products.

Sheri Rose Shepherd
P.O. Box 3500 Suite 227
Sisters, OR 97759

or visit her on the Web at
www.sherirose.com